A HOUSE WITH NO ROOF

A HOUSE WITH

WITH

AFTER MY
FATHER'S ASSASSINATION,
A MEMOIR

NO ROOF

REBECCA WILSON

COUNTERPOINT
BERKELEY

Introduction copyright © 2011 Anne Lamott

Author's note: This is a memoir of actual events and real people. I have, however,
used some of the techniques of fiction in order to tell the story most accurately and
honestly, based upon my memory and my research. I have also changed some of the
names to protect the privacy of others. I am indebted to: "The Trade Union Murders"
by Joe Gores, *Blood Brotherhood* by John Van Der Zee; the Labor Archives and
Research Center at San Francisco State University; Bryan Lambert for the investigative
report; and Pat Wright for the folio of clippings.

Library of Congress Cataloging-in-Publication Data

Wilson, Rebecca E.
A house with no roof : after my father's assassination : a memoir / Rebecca Wilson ;
[introduction by] Anne Lamott.
p. cm.
ISBN 978-1-58243-754-5 (pbk.)
1. Wilson, Rebecca E. 2. Children of murder victims—California—Biography. 3.
Murder—California—Case studies. 4. Fathers—Death—Psychological aspects. 5.
Loss (Psychology) I. Title.
HV6533.C2W55 2011
362.88—dc22
[B]
2011012433

Cover design by Anna Bauer
Interior design by www.meganjonesdesign.com

COUNTERPOINT
1919 Fifth Street
Berkeley, CA 94710

www.counterpointpress.com
Distributed by Publishers Group West
Printed in the United States of America

For Malcolm
&
For Annie

CONTENTS

SF UNION LEADER SHOT DEAD

Dow Wilson, 40, bearded and militant leader of the
2500-member housepainters union here, was killed
by two shotgun blasts early yesterday . . .

. . . the slain union officer, who lived in an upstairs flat
at 121 Seventh Avenue, left a widow, Barbara, and
three children, Lee, 18, Amalia, 14, and Rebecca, 3.

—FROM AN ARTICLE BY CHARLES RAUDEBAUGH,
SAN FRANCISCO CHRONICLE, APRIL 6, 1966

A HOUSE WITH NO ROOF

INTRODUCTION BY ANNE LAMOTT

I T IS A pleasure to introduce you to Rebecca Wilson, whose brave and marvelous book you hold in your hands. Rebecca's mother was a friend to my father as he was dying thirty years ago, and her mother's illness two years later brought me to Rebecca's side, and placed me forever in her orbit.

Rebecca was one of those young girls who stood out in the physically glorious, psychologically ingrown town of Bolinas, where we all lived during the late sixties and the seventies. Everyone in town knew everyone else. She was unusually self-possessed, which I attributed to her prowess on and love for her horse, and she had a shy, elegant beauty not of this era. I noticed her at a young age, running with other girls across the fields and beaches of the area, sometimes on horses and sometimes on foot. I was ten years older, and knew little about her then—I knew her father had been assassinated in San Francisco when she was three, which was five or six years before we met. I also knew her dashing and dangerous older brother, with whom I frequently played tennis. And years later I came to know her mother, Barbara, who was extraordinary in her brilliance, artistic eccentricities, and ferocious, plainspoken feminism. And who, as you will read, could be impossible.

But I didn't really *know* Rebecca until her mother's monstrous fight with cancer, which began when Rebecca was barely sixteen. Rebecca seemed to most of us in town to be in charge. Where was her brother, where was the grown-up sister? Those of us who stepped in to help care for Barbara only had hints of family damage that was so extensive that only the teenager would stay in Bolinas, close to the mother. During those days, we all pretended to be free of opinion or judgment of other people's behavior when it came to freedom and detachment from old family bonds.

The cost of mothering such a sick and needy mother would have been the end of most teenagers' dreams and confidence, and it almost was for Rebecca. Instead, shouldering the burden of a tragic family at such a fraught and vulnerable stage in life became the beginning of a lifelong search for self, for home and wholeness and a healed soul.

This is the story she tells in *A House with No Roof*.

Rebecca is blessed with a gentle nature, a sly sense of humor, and an astonishing ability to describe nature. She writes in strong, clean, and often surprising prose about her girlhood—about her father's murder, about becoming a teenager with a mother who needed her to be the parent, about growing into a woman of extraordinary clarity, delicious depths, great humor, quiet insight.

I believe this lushness inside Rebecca springs from the richness of who she is—from her ability to pay attention and capture exactly each painful, joyful, or shocking moment of remembering, becoming, recapturing, intuiting, chasing down temporary relief, casting off falsehood. Nature, her friend and lover (often found in the form of horses and wolf-dogs), and time have so honed her that she never needs to exaggerate. She has ridden herself of the stuff not needed and what is not true so that what remains is as authentic and wild as a garden.

Rebecca is absolutely one of the most trustworthy people I know, and paradoxically, this quality, along with her watchfulness and calmness, are what make this book so exciting. It's a deeply touching story of spirit, of whatever thrust helps us keep moving forward, and of the sweetness and sorrow of families. It is all of our stories, in fact—of survival, transcendence, defeat, resurrection. Who on earth are we, really? Who were these strange and difficult parents of ours, and who are we without them? How do we find ourselves and our purposes here in the swirls of our crazy lives? What is real, and how do we move forward from terrible loss and destruction into the potential for wonder, for true presence and adventure and love? How do we find our way, let alone truth and beauty, playfulness and resilience, amidst the mess of our heartaches, thrills, diversions? How do we stay sane when everything we've known has been so fraught with difficult parents, with lies, addiction, and madness?

I think her story will blow you away.

Rebecca Wilson's is a new voice in American letters, at once pure and heartfelt, rough and jaunty. She's a natural storyteller with an amazing story that she tells with plainness and eloquence. I don't quite know how she pulled this off, but I love and admire this book, as I do its author. I believe you will, too.

1 · FRACTURED

SINCE WE DON'T talk about our mom, and we can't talk about our dad, I'm shocked when my sister calls to ask me to go with her to dig up Dad's ashes. She tells me she got the map from the man who'd helped Mom bury them all those years ago, the man who says he knows *exactly* where they put them.

"And," Amalia says, "I need you to help me."

Driving to Muir Beach on the Northern California coast, we're both anxious, each wary of the other. And so we do what we always do when we're together and making the other one nervous:

"*Respect!* Just a little bit!" We're shouting along with Aretha, who is blaring out of the speakers.

We have the gardening trowels stowed in the trunk of Amalia's car and a wooden box for the ashes. I'm twenty-eight years old, and she is thirty-nine, eleven years older.

A light rain is falling as we arrive. We hover uncertainly in the parking lot. The dirt path before us zigzags downhill about a quarter of a mile, between abandoned WWII bunkers, down some steps, then out to a fenced overlook at the edge of a cliff. Just beyond this point, the land drops away sharply, straight into the ocean. We cannot see the waves, but we can hear them below, breaking against the jagged cliffs. The air tastes wet and salty and smells like sage. From this point, on a clear day, you can see all the way to San Francisco.

Amalia unfolds the hand-drawn map and points to a rocky outcropping on a small hillock about halfway down, off the left side of the path.

"See? That's where Dad is," she says. "Near those rocks." Amalia shoves me forward. "Okay, you go first."

"No, *you* go," I shove her back. "This was *your* idea."

We each laugh nervously. Amalia takes a deep breath and reaches out for me. "Okay," she says, "Let's go together."

We hold on to the railing, cold metal, slick with rain. We swing ourselves over it, then climb up through the bushes, coyote brush and sage, threaded with poison oak.

"What are we looking for?" I ask.

Amalia frowns at the map. "There's a brass plaque cemented to one of these rocks, with Dad's initials etched on it. That's where the ashes are." She points. "There, but it's probably hidden by all these bushes."

"Come on," she adds. "We have to start somewhere."

We begin to pull away branches and to poke vaguely with our trowels at the dirt around the base of the rocks.

"What are we looking for, an urn?" I ask.

"Not an urn—the guy said it's just this red Folgers coffee can, with a plastic top."

"No shit!"

"Yeah. But probably the jumbo size, no? For their great, big, giant-sized union leader."

"Yeah," I say. "Would have to be the super-saver."

I run my hand along the rocks, and my fingers catch on something rough, a layer of old cement on the smooth rock face. I chip at it with my trowel, breaking off a tiny piece. I trace the edges with my fingers. It's a gray square, but the plaque—with our father's name—has been pried away.

"Hey," I say, "I think this might be it, but the plaque's gone."

Amalia leaps up.

"Right here! Feel it," I say. We are quiet for a moment.

"If this is it—" she says.

". . . then we're standing on him," I say.

We clutch the trowels to our chests and look down.

"Hello," a voice calls out, startling us. There's a woman on the path above us. She's gray-haired, and a man stands behind her, tugging on her arm.

"Stop, Henry," she says. "I'm trying to talk to these girls. What are you doing down there?" she asks.

Mortified, I bend over and pretend to dig while Amalia nervously stands up, wiping her hands on her jeans.

"Well," she says, "We're just digging up our father."

"Your father! Henry, these girls say they're trying to exhume their father's body."

"No," Amalia tells her. "His ashes. Our mother buried him here, but there's no tombstone—and we," she waves her hand in the air, "We'd like to move him, you know? To somewhere better . . . ?"

"Well, now," the woman said. "Maybe we can help, my husband's a minister. He can say a prayer for your father."

"Frances, will you please come along," Henry says quietly. "These girls need to be left alone."

Amalia and I stare after them, then burst out laughing, tears springing from our eyes.

"Prayers," I choke. "Just what our dad, the agnostic anarchist, would want and really *need.*"

"Oh, my God!" Amalia says, wiping her cheeks. "This is crazy. What was I thinking?"

"No idea," I say. "Where were you planning on putting him, anyway? Maybe just let him ride around in the trunk for a while, until you figured it out? '*Oh, jeez,*'" I say. "'Will you *look* at that? Dad spilled all over that spare tire again!'"

"Shit," Amalia laughs. "Let's get the hell out of here."

We do; we leave. We leave Dad there. But I don't want to—I'm sad, and I'm not exactly sure we've really found him.

Years later, the night before my fifteen-year-old wolf-dog, Max, died, he and I slept on the deck outside our home in Northern California, as I talked to him about his life.

"Remember when you ripped the fence out? And the hole you ate in the bedroom door? And when you killed the neighbor's chicken?"

We lay facing each other: Max, on a red-striped, foam doggie bed; me, in my blue sleeping bag on thin air mattresses I'd borrowed, two days past my forty-sixth birthday. I put my hands on his face.

"It has been so exciting to live with you," I told him as he fell into a deep rhythmic breathing. "You are the most beautiful thing I have ever seen."

Then I told him our best beach story: Once, after a winter storm, I took Max and his wolfy sister, Chau, to the shore by the Point Bonita Lighthouse at the opening of San Francisco Bay. They raced down the cliff to the water, and a huge wave swept them up and out to sea. They paddled frantically, noses held high, their wide yellow eyes fixed on me. The next big wave washed them back onto the sand, and they raced to me, barking madly, joyfully.

I recited for Max bits from Rudyard Kipling's "How the Elephant Got His Trunk": "On the great grey-green, greasy Limpopo River, all set about with fever trees . . ." Mostly, I kept repeating, "Oh Best Beloved, oh Best Beloved."

A psychic once told me that Max was my father reincarnated. He'd come back so late in my life because it took him a while to figure out what shape to come in so he could best protect me. Also, he had no wish to be murdered again. We dozed a little, my hands in his ruff. As always, Max was so generous with me, giving me time to say goodbye.

I HAVE ONLY one picture of my family: it was taken during our second life, the one that began when our father was killed.

A Polaroid, taken in July 1969, in front of our new house in the tiny beach community of Bolinas, not far from Muir Beach. My mother, Barbara, is forty-five; my brother, Lee, twenty-one; and my sister, Amalia, seventeen. I'm the little one, only six years old. The adults drape their arms around each other. Everyone but Lee is dressed up to go out—he's in shorts and a shirt, his feet bare, one foot resting atop the other. Mom has on a plum-colored dress from the 1930s, with matching stockings and shoes. Amalia wears an ankle-length beaver coat over a red velvet dress. Behind them, barely visible, are the legs and tail of our dog, Puppers.

What you can't see is the front deck of our house, with my red and white jungle gym and the rust-covered refrigerator, its freezer stuffed with cartons of my brother's favorite banana-walnut and carob-flavored ice creams that I am forbidden by him from eating.

We face into the sun. I'm wearing a short pink dress, white knee-high socks, and white shoes, and clutching a bouquet of wild sweet peas. My long hair is a tangle, and one front tooth is missing. Amalia and Lee both have their eyes nearly closed, and there's a slackness in their faces that makes me guess they're stoned. My mother is wearing dark glasses. You can tell from our hair and the bend of the tall weeds around us that this is a windy day.

We are a family of strong personalities, those who know how to fill a room. My brother, the drug smuggler; my sister, the musician; and my flamboyant mother, who was afraid of the dark and slept with the light on. Me. My aunt Kate, my father's sister, is in the picture, too. You can't see it, but I know she's wearing her favorite pendant, which reads, "War is not healthy for children and other living things." I think of her as a placeholder for Dad. We're posing earnestly, like normal people. But, truth be told, my father's murder fractured the family and set us madly in some motion that we've never stopped.

My relatives always told me I was too young when he died to have any memories, but I do remember him. I recall the Labor Temple in San Francisco, where he held me in his arms during union meetings as he paced before the members, whose voices were raised in anger and debate. His dark beard smelled of sweet pipe tobacco and tickled my face when he kissed me, his sweater soft under my hands. And when he spoke or laughed, the sound reverberated through me.

My father, Dow Wilson, was a union official, Recording Secretary of San Francisco Local No. 4 of the Brotherhood of Painters, Decorators and Paperhangers of America.

He was a political radical, an incorruptible leader of men, famous because he could not be bought. A series of clashes with a corrupt union official named Ben Rasnick led to my father's assassination.

In 1965, during a Northern California painters' strike, he and fifty of his men broke into a Sacramento union meeting where officials were making a secret settlement with contractors. Shouting "Sellout!" and "Rat fink!" Dad's men dragged Rasnick, the East Bay District Council Secretary, out of the meeting. Enraged, Rasnick filed misconduct charges against my father, for behavior unbecoming a union official, charges that were eventually dropped.

In 1966, when the Sacramento Painters Union discovered that nearly a quarter of a million dollars was missing from their welfare fund, they came to my father. With his help, they began secretly gathering evidence. When the missing money was linked to Rasnick, my father publicly called for both an investigation and an internal audit—it was then that he began being threatened by anonymous phone calls. But my parents were used to this; both were labor organizers and considered themselves class warriors. Neither was faint of heart. On evenings when Dad was out on union business, my mom answered the door with his shotgun in hand.

On an April night, after a members' meeting at the
Labor Temple, Dad went across the street to the B&E
Tavern on Sixteenth Street, talking with a couple of his
men until nearly one, then walked to his car, parked
several blocks away on South Van Ness. Two men were
parked near where he was unlocking the car. He was shot
twice: one blast striking him in the chest, the other, in his
head.

My father died there on the pavement of that San
Francisco street, at one in the morning on the fifth of April,
1966. South Van Ness then was much as it is today, a mix
of residences, auto dealerships, small shops, seedy transient
hotels, Mexican restaurants.

My father was forty years old. Amalia was fourteen,
Lee, eighteen. I was three and a half, the baby. Mom was
forty-two. She held me on her lap, stroked my hair, said my
dad wasn't coming home. She told me he'd been killed by
robbers—the baby's version of the truth. I cried: The robbers had stolen him from our lives.

One month after Dad was gunned down, a second union
leader was slain. No one knew who the assassins were, nor
who would be next, but now there were men from the union
acting as our bodyguards. Grief and instinct told my mother
to run. Lee fought her and refused to come; he stayed in
San Francisco on his own. Mom took Amalia and me and
drove night and day until we reached Guadalajara, Mexico,
where my parents had hidden during the McCarthy Era, to

avoid being subpoenaed by the House Committee on Un-American Activities.

Mom knew an American man who ran an orphanage for Mexican children where we could hide. We lived in a small house inside the orphanage walls. In this terrible place, dirty, paint peeling off the walls, weeks slowly passed. We sometimes ate in the dining hall at the orphanage. The cook was named Clementina, and on her birthday, after dinner, I climbed barefoot onto a wooden table—I'm told—and sang to a crowded hall, "Oh my darling Clementine / you are lost and gone forever / dreadful sorry, Clementine." The people roared, stomped, shaking the table on which I stood.

It was three months before we came back to California, to Echo Park, called "Red Hill," in Los Angeles, where my parents had leftist friends. Mom was still very depressed and sad. She often left us alone in the house, or other times she'd lock herself in her bedroom and weep, or she'd be stoned on Valium, or become crazily acting-out manic. Amalia never went out to buy drugs in Echo Park; she only had to open up Mom's medicine cabinet, filled with vials of uppers and downers. It was later when Amalia told me, "I used to help myself."

Two of the communist families there, the Goreks and the Poteets, had kids. The Goreks had five children; the Poteets, three. Mom called us all "the red diaper babies."

Mom planted rows of cheerful purple and yellow pansies in front of our house. On her hands and knees in the heat, she sweated and swore as she dug holes in the dry and hard-packed dirt: exhausting labor, but nothing offered real relief. She was always frightened, always. She planted them, found no catharsis for her grief, became distracted. Mom would forget to water, and her pansies always died.

LEFT ON OUR own and unsupervised, we roamed our neighborhood, a warren of steep staircases and narrow pathways that led from house to house, street to street. Away from the eyes of adults, the days began with the ritual of The Butt Check Club, our version of playing doctor. The bigger kids made the little ones stand in a row, pull down our pants, and bend over. Then they went down the line, checking each of our butts to make sure that we'd wiped ourselves. Punishment for a dirty butt was a spanking by the older kids and the humiliation of having to wear your skid-marked underpants inside out all day long.

Then we'd spy on our landlord's wife, Mrs. Feingold, who was a nudist. She'd lounge in her backyard on an old couch, a transistor radio tuned to the local jazz station, her martini and coconut oil propped on a small wooden box. She'd come out her back door, clad only in a towel, turn slowly in a circle, lowering the towel little by little, like a stripper, before dropping it and lying down on her back. We'd hide in the bushes, peering, taking turns, and swatting at the large red ants that crawled up our legs, biting us, leaving quarter-sized welts.

We were not allowed to leave our hill, Vestal Street the uphill boundary, and Preston Avenue downhill, and the cross-streets of Ewing and Baker. It was 1967. There were riots and civil rights demonstrations at nearby Belmont High School, and the students who demonstrated were beaten and jailed. Amalia hung out with a pack of teenagers, including Luis, a tall, handsome Latino, and two white guys with long hair who called themselves Rough and Ready. They'd come to our house to hang out, smoke dope, listen to Donovan. Ready showed up one morning with his arm in a cast.

"How'd you break your arm?" I asked.

"Running from the cops." He paused and took a long drag off the joint. "I climbed up onto the roof and tried to jump to the next building." Ready blew smoke out his mouth and grinned. "Almost made it, man."

My mother bought a red Volkswagen Bug. She liked to drive Amalia and me to a hilltop where we'd watch the sun sink in an orange and pink sky. She loved to watch these L.A. sunsets—the colors, she said, were caused by smog.

On our drive down the hill one evening, a neighbor's dog jumped into the street in front of us, and there was this terrible thump. I looked out the rear window and saw the dog lying motionless, also people yelling and waving at us.

"Stop!" I screamed. "You hurt that dog!"

Mom kept going.

"We have to go back!" Amalia yelled.

"I can't, I can't," my mother said. "If I don't stop, they'll never know who did it."

"What?" Amalia shrieked. "We live three blocks from here!"

My mother stepped on the accelerator. "What am I supposed to do? Go back and say, 'Sorry, I'm the one who ran over your dog?'"

When she was especially sad, she didn't shop for groceries. She often forgot to eat, and grew thin. Those times, Amalia and I went to Mrs. Poteet's.

"Come on in, kids," she'd yell from her chair, where she was watching television. "Are you hungry? There's dinner on the stove—help yourselves."

We'd make our way through the chairs covered with piles of unfolded laundry and the stacks of unread newspapers and magazines that lined the hallway, into her warm, dirty kitchen. Amalia would scoop up plates of simmering beans or tuna casserole, and we'd go sit on the floor next to Mrs. Poteet to eat.

Lee had been living in San Francisco. Mom decided it was time for him to come home, be fed, clothed, for him to become part of the family again. In preparation, she went to the local flea market and bought seven antique cut-crystal bowls. The night he got home, she made chicken soup for our celebration dinner. We watched her ladle it into the first bowl, which cracked in half, spilling the soup all over the stove. Wordlessly, she picked up another bowl and ladled more soup into it. It split too. Again she tried; again, it cracked into pieces. A sea of steaming chicken noodle soup spread across the floor.

When she ran out of bowls, she turned to face us, waved the ladle in the air, and announced, "There will be no dinner tonight!" Then she walked into her bedroom and slammed the door.

THE TIMES MY mother was focused, she'd carefully teach me something practical, like how to cut the top off a soft-boiled egg. One day she brought me the girl puppy we called Puppers. Mom said a dog would make our house feel more like home. Amalia brought home three kittens, one black, two calicos. She named the black kitten Pocahontas, and together, we named the others Midiface and Wilma Flintstone.

Mom hated her own name, Barbara. She hated her childhood nickname even more, and forbade me to call her Barbie. "I am *not* some fucking anatomically incorrect doll," she'd say.

Her blue eyes were nearsighted, so she always wore thick glasses with tortoiseshell frames. She had a little lady's mustache and used to tease, "Before I married your father, I was the Bearded Lady in a circus." Her favorite swear word was *motherfucker*.

Some nights—her good nights—Mom would tell me a story or read one from a book. There was a real-life story she liked to tell about me too, and I never tired of hearing it, of how I had defied my nursery school teacher and led the kids outside, and the teacher had had to call my mother to take me home.

She'd laugh and say, "Becky, sometimes you are just so much like your father." She meant rebellious, outrageous, and brave.

When she told this story, later, she was being soft and easy with me. But in those first years after his murder, Mom was undone and often swung between extreme moods, either grieving or radiating bravado. And I began to dream the dream I've dreamed all my life: masked men on a dark street, sharp flashes of light.

2 · WILSONS ARE BOLD

MOM BOUGHT LAND in Bolinas, an artists' community on the coast, in west Marin County. To get there you drive north across the Golden Gate Bridge from San Francisco, take the Stinson Beach/Highway 1 exit. Highway 1 splits into two highways: Panoramic Highway runs over Mount Tamalpais, and Shoreline Highway runs along the coast through Muir Beach. Both highways converge in Stinson Beach and continue north as Highway 1, following the edge of Bolinas Lagoon. At the lagoon's tip, you turn left on Olema-Bolinas Road and drive two miles to downtown Bolinas. If you miss the turn, the next town north is Dogtown, population 20.

MONEY FROM SOME union contributions and a small lawsuit she'd won from an insurance company would build us a house in Bolinas and allow us start our new life.

I was five when she packed us into our Volkswagen Bug, with its four-cylinder engine in back and tiny trunk in front. Amalia's three cats in a carrying cage were wedged, among other belongings, under the hood in front. When the hood wouldn't close, Mom ran a chain around the front bumper and through its handle. She padlocked the chain, and we drove off, out of L.A. and up Interstate 5 toward San Francisco. We must have been quite a sight. Cars pulled beside us to gape at the overstuffed little automobile, with smoke belching out the back, cats yowling and clawing desperately to get out the front, where the wind poured in.

"You're going to *love* Bolinas," Mom told us as we drove the winding Panoramic Highway over Mount Tamalpais for the first time. "It's full of writers, poets, painters, sculptors—everyone's a bohemian."

Downtown Bolinas lay between the mouth of the lagoon to the east, the Pacific Ocean to the west, and behind it, the Mesa, dotted with houses. The dirty main street ran east and west, ending at the beach. We drove past funky Victorian homes, a shabby tennis court, a liquor store, a Laundromat, a realty office, two churches, a gas station, the town's community center, a restaurant, a general store, and a saloon. Mangy dogs, with bandannas tied around their necks, trotted down the street, some missing legs. The pack followed a bare-chested, barefoot man in tattered white bell-bottoms and neckties knotted around his thighs, ankles, and upper arms. One was tied around his forehead, its ends hanging down over an ear.

"Let's go see our house," my mother said.

We drove up Terrace Road to the Mesa. There were only three paved roads running the length of it, and the crossroads were potholed dirt tracks, named alphabetically: Aspen, Birch, Cedar, Dogwood, Evergreen, Fern. Our house was at the corner of Alder and Iris.

We bounced down a dirt road, passing a group of barefoot kids with long, snarly hair and grubby faces, the littlest child—a girl—wore nothing but underpants.

The Bug lurched to a stop. Mom got out and opened her arms. "Ta *daaa*," she sang out.

Amalia, Lee, and I climbed out and stood staring. Before us was the skeletal frame of a two-story house supported on huge cement posts. A long wooden walk connected the driveway to the deck. The house had no walls or roof, only the ladder that connected the first floor to the second.

Amalia pointed to a large, squarish thing wrapped in a black plastic tarp on the second floor. A corner of the tarp flapped in the breeze. "What is that?"

"That," Mother said, "is the piano. We had to put it in first, before we built the stairs—"

"Mom! Look!" I pointed to a man who popped up from behind the piano. He was tall and skinny, and fringed with long, greasy hair. He swept the tarp off and ran his fingers along the keys, closed his eyes, and—head back—launched into a classical piece. We listened respectfully—he was good.

"He's playing Chopin," Amalia told me.

Abruptly, he stopped and turned toward us. Mother cupped her hands around her mouth. "Who are you?" she shouted.

"Who are *you?*" the man shouted back.

My mother planted her fists on her hips. "THIS IS *MY* HOUSE," she said.

"Oh! Well, okay then. This is a very good piano, you know. You really shouldn't leave it out here like this, in a house with no roof, no walls to protect it. It's too fine an instrument to be left to warp in the forces of wind and rain and fog. My name is Abner Galloway. I am a concert pianist." He bowed deeply.

"Of course you are," my mother said.

"I shall play a song of welcome for you to your new house." He crouched over the keyboard, flexed his fingers, and played again. When he finished, my mother clapped politely.

"Thank you, Abner. That was very nice."

He stood and bowed again, carefully covered the piano, climbed down the ladder, and swung himself off the deck. He stepped into the bushes and disappeared.

"So, what do you think?" Mom said.

WHILE CONSTRUCTION WAS being finished, we moved to Mill Valley on the other side of Mount Tamalpais. There we lived in a cavernous, dark Victorian house. I was five, Amalia was sixteen, and Lee was twenty. We moved in, and I went out walking and promptly got lost, ending up at the police station in town. My mother was furious. She picked me up, and when we got around the corner from the station, she made me hand over the lollipop a policeman had given me.

"Why did you go to the police? We don't *ever* go to the police," she said.

When I think of that house, I remember it as filled with ghosts. It's there my brother started shooting heroin. Amalia walked in on Lee shooting up in the bathroom. When she informed our mother, Mom slapped her across the face and told her to shut up.

But trouble came with us to our brand-new home in Bolinas. Lee was handsome, with our father's dark, curly hair. When Lee pursed his lips, his face resembled Robert Redford's, with the same thin lips and narrowing of the eyes. Soon after we moved in, Lee began bringing girlfriends home. His girlfriends were all beautiful, with long hair or large afros, all slow-speaking women, with names like Mandy and Sugar—they'd follow him around the house and out into the back bedroom, sometimes walking down the hall to the bathroom naked. All the while, Mom, jaw shut tight, clattered dishes in the sink and banged the kitchen drawers hard.

But Mom was determined to start her new life. She began "making art," as she called it. A four-foot purple angel she constructed from plaster of Paris and cheesecloth hung from the ceiling in the living room, which was two stories high. Halfway up the stairs, a small landing overlooked the living room. My mother envisioned Amalia getting married in that living room, walking down those stairs as we all watched from below. In the meantime, she hung the angel in the air, just off the landing.

Our living room was where Amalia practiced her flute and danced to the records of Aretha Franklin, Janis Joplin, the Supremes. She taught me the Mashed Potato, the Swim, the Loco-Motion. She was beautiful, the only blond in our family—tall and voluptuous. When we danced, I followed behind her and tried to imitate her turns, the way her body swayed, the lift of her graceful arms.

In the downstairs bathroom, Mother painted an American flag on the lid of the toilet seat. On one wall, she hung twenty-five hand-carved wooden decoy ducks that had belonged to my father, an avid duck hunter. In the upstairs bathroom, she suspended a ceramic casting of a deflated hot water bottle with a small banner across it that read WOMEN'S LIBERATION. She wrote notes to herself on the mirror there in pink lipstick. These ranged from shopping reminders, like "get milk," to quotations: "If you are afraid to tell the truth, then you don't deserve the freedom. Malcolm X."

Mom sewed a twelve-foot banner with big black letters that read WILSONS ARE BOLD. She made a flagpole out of a small eucalyptus tree trunk, nailed it to the front deck, and flew the banner over our house. When my two new friends, Kara and Ruby, came over for the first time, they stared up it.

"What does that mean?" Ruby asked.

"I don't know," I replied. "My mom says it's *art.*"

Mom let our yard run to weeds till it was indistinguishable from the rest of the Mesa, a wilderness of coyote brush, blackberry vines, orange and yellow nasturtiums, stands of hemlock, and wild plum, fir, eucalyptus, and pine trees. Bevies of quail ran in front of cars, zigzagging in panic before lifting off. At night, raccoons ventured onto our deck to eat any dog food left out and to raid our garbage cans.

BOLINAS WAS WILD, a hip place to live. Artists mixed with Portuguese ranching families, with rednecks and creative eccentrics. Up the road from us lived the son and grandson of Philo Farnsworth, who had invented the television. Beat Poets and writers showed up to hang out or live for a time. People like Robert Creeley and his wife, Bobbie Louise Hawkins; Lawrence Ferlinghetti; Bill Berkson; Joanne Kyger; Jim Carroll; and Richard Brautigan. Artists and activists and freethinkers of all kinds came: painters, sculptors, ecologists, filmmakers, folksingers, and rock stars.

The town seemed to welcome crazy people, such as Pickett the Dog Man with his pack of three-legged dogs, and the pianist we'd met the first day, Abner Galloway, who really had been a famous concert pianist before he lost his mind. We called people like this "burnouts." There were other singular, but less threatening, characters: Mad May, daughter of a famous painter, who liked to jump out in front of bikes and cars, and Towering Eagle and his girlfriend, Horizon, who walked by our house every day, chanting harmonies of the Sanskrit word *om*, drawing the word out, *ooommmmm*, and Elias, the self-proclaimed preacher who wore a long velvet cape when he rode his white horse across the Mesa. And more.

When my mother talked about them all, she shook her head, laughed, and said, "There's a direct line between the state mental hospital and Bolinas, California. When they let the crazy people out of Napa, they come *directly* here."

When I began to write as a young woman, I was afraid. My role models were mostly arrogant, drunk, crazy, broke, usually unlikable.

I thought that to write, you'd need to be willing to lose your mind.

KARA, RUBY, AND I were best friends. We dug in the sand at Agate Beach for smooth red, green, and blue agates and the brighter shards of bottle-green and blue beach sea glass. At low tide, we'd walk carefully along the edges of tide pools, looking for hermit crabs, sea snails, and starfish in pink, orange, red, and purple. We'd gently poke sea anemones to feel them close slowly over our fingers, like soft, cold mouths. When the tide came in, we waited as long as we dared before running back to shore.

Kara lived up the road from my family, in a house hidden deep within a small eucalyptus forest. Her father was the architect who designed our house, and her mother was a poet. She had an older brother and sister. Her mom was strict about chores and meal times: Each child had to help cook dinner once a week, and they ate dinner at seven every night.

Ruby, Kara, and I loved to run through Kara's eucalyptus forest, hiding from each other and the witches and ghosts we believed floated in the darkness beneath the trees.

Ruby's family had moved to Bolinas from New York City. They lived on Ocean Parkway in a flat cinder block house at the edge of a cliff. Their living room faced the ocean, and the front of their house was all windows. On clear days, from their living room, you could see all the way to San Francisco. They had the biggest color television I had ever seen—which was always on. Her dad was a doctor. Ruby had a twin brother named Oliver and an older brother and sister.

Ruby's mom, Hannah, was small, round, kind. Hannah chain-smoked and wore tentlike dresses. She was always in the kitchen, smoking and cooking, also forever joining

Weight Watchers. Their open kitchen shelves were packed with bags of puffed rice cereal, cans of soup, matzo crackers, jars of peanut butter and jelly. If we got hungry, we were allowed to help ourselves. We loved hanging out at Ruby's house because there was always something going on and we were always welcome.

Ruby's parents fought a lot. Her mom and dad would argue, and the kids would join in, Ruby yelling at everyone else to stop yelling. Their dog would bark, somebody would slam a door, and no one ever remembered to turn the television off. Ruby said they were loud and fought like that because they were *New Yorkers*. New Yorkers always yell, she said, but will always make up afterward.

Sometimes we three coasted our bikes downhill into town. Terrace Road wound along the cliff, then through a sprawling eucalyptus grove, and alongside an overlook where the surfers parked to clock the waves. Every summer and fall, monarch butterflies migrated to this eucalyptus forest. Their arrival was beautiful, miraculous: They covered the leaves, transforming the silver and green forest into a living sea of orange and black—thousands of delicate wings, opening and closing. When they died, the road was literally covered with their wings.

When we got Downtown, we'd pass the community center, which housed the town's Free Box and a small library, and go to the Bolinas General Store to buy candy, or popsicles. Next to the store was a vacant dirt lot—once the site of Tarantino's Seafood Restaurant, rumored to have been torched for insurance money—now, filled with litter, weeds, dog shit. Across from the store stood Smiley's Schooner Saloon. We crossed the street rather than walk in front of Smiley's, as we were afraid someone we knew— a drunk mother or father—would call out to us and we wouldn't know what to say or do.

Downtown was a funky place, the spaces between buildings lush with overgrowth, what sidewalks there were, uneven. There was a bulletin board on the front of the store, a kind of public classifieds. As children, we were a little wary, afraid we'd be accosted by the burnouts hanging out. We felt watched—there was always an undercurrent, slightly hostile, brooding—and we never stayed long.

Instead, we gravitated to the small wharf at the mouth of the lagoon. At low tide, we waded across to Kent Island, where, in the shallows, small leopard sharks nibbled our toes. In the warm months of September and October, we swam in the cold Pacific, swimming as close to the harbor seals as they'd let us, diving and rolling in the waves, pretending we were seals ourselves.

From Downtown, we'd hitch a ride, tossing our bikes into the back of a passing pickup truck back to the top of the Mesa, then ride our bikes home. In the winter, the Mesa roads turned into mud slicks, the potholes becoming giant puddles. We played in the largest ones, cupping pollywogs in our hands and, a little while later, tiny frogs.

AT SCHOOL, COOTIE KISSERS was the big game during recess and lunchtime. It was simple: Girls chased boys around the swings and tried to kiss them. Most only threatened to kiss the boys, but I really did it. I caught Tommy and pinned him.

"Yuck! Get off me!" Tommy yelled, batting his hands at my nose.

The kids screamed, "Kiss him! Kiss him! Kiss him again!"

"Becky! Get off Tommy right now!" Mrs. Jorgensen, our teacher, shouted, hauling me off by my collar.

"What is going on here?"

"Cootie Kissers," I said.

"Becky's the queen of the Cootie Kissers," one of the kids said. "She was giving Tommy cooties."

"Becky and Tommy, inside, right now," Mrs. Jorgensen said. In the classroom, she opened the large coat closet in the back of the room. "Get in, both of you."

We did, and she slammed the door shut.

"Maybe this will teach you," she said through the door. "You stay in there until lunch is over, until I come for you."

Embarrassed and suddenly shy, Tommy and I retreated to opposite ends, hands behind our backs. We were quiet, listening to each other breathe, waiting for the bell to ring, signaling the end of lunch period.

Later that week, Mrs. Jorgensen announced that if our class was good, we would be allowed to join the third graders for Mrs. Crenshaw's afternoon music class.

Mrs. Crenshaw had long, straight brown hair. She wore miniskirts, brown suede go-go boots, love beads. I had never seen a teacher like her. She didn't holler, she singsonged. She taught us the words to "The Ballad of Davy Crockett," playing the autoharp while we sang along. I completely adored her.

In our second class session with her, she told us, "Today we are going learn something very special, the Pledge of Allegiance. It is the oath that we say every day as citizens, pledging our minds, hearts, and souls to this great democracy, America. Shall we recite the pledge now?"

Afterward, I raised my hand. "Mrs. Crenshaw, what are you if you believe in liberty and justice for all?"

Her smile faded a little. "Becky, what a question! Let's see, if you believe in liberty, then you're a liberal. The word *liberal* comes from the word *liberty*," she explained, smiling brightly again.

"How was school?" my mother asked as we drove home.

"Good. We learned the Pledge of Allegiance."

"Hummph."

"Mom," I said, "when I grow up, I want to be a liberal."

My mother pulled over to the side of the road and turned to face me.

"We are not liberals," she said. "Liberals talk about helping the poor people, the blacks, the Mexicans, the farm workers, the women, they even *cry* about it, that's why they call them bleeding hearts. But they never do anything—we *do* things. Do you understand me?"

"Yes," I said.

"Good," she said and slipped the car into gear.

The next day, Mrs. Jorgensen sent me to the closet again because I refused to do the pledge.

THOUGH I WAS afraid of the dark like my mom, I liked closets. The dark of night felt ominous, vast, and I had trouble falling asleep, often reading myself to sleep. My mother did not usually let me sleep with her because I'd keep her awake with my sleep-talking and kicking.

But the darkness of closets was small, protective. I liked my mother's closet; there, I felt invisible. When she was not home and I was scared, I'd get in her closet and shut the door. Crouching on top of her shoes, I'd close my eyes. The darkness smelled like her, and I felt safe. There, I thought about my dad sometimes. I imagined he missed me, and that he wanted to come back to us.

Mostly, what happened to Dad seemed like a black-and-white movie, distant and flat; events that happened over there, away from me. But sometimes I remembered fragments: my sister keening; the feeling of being very cold, like I was falling and falling; the front steps of our house at 121 Seventh Avenue in the Inner Richmond District of San Francisco, tiled in a black-and-white mosaic; two men dragging a half-conscious Lee up those same stairs and into the house, his head falling forward on his chest; somber men in suits standing guard over us in front of the house; up the street, the immense green of the Presidio; and before Dad died, taking baths with Amalia, singing and scrubbing each other's backs. I remembered these things while in the dark of the closet.

I asked my mom if there was a funeral, and she said no, but there was a memorial at the Labor Temple—and thousands of people came.

"Was I there?" I asked.

"No," she said. "You were so little we left you with friends."

"Did I cry when Dad died?" I asked her another time.

"Oh, yes, I used to take you to the playground, and you'd swing on the swings and cry and cry. And you listened to your record, *The Story of Babar, the Little Elephant*, over and over, and when the hunters shot Babar's mother, you cried."

This talk of my dad's death made me both eager and terrified; stories about his murder came in flashes and shocks, often by accident. Stories of his life were more complete, told to me over and over again, like favorite bedtime stories. Even now, his absence is a mystery. Sometimes I feel ridiculous in my curiosity, like the baby bird from the story *Are You My Mother?* except I ask, *Did you know my father?*

But I want to run away from it, for fear—if I come too close—his death will swallow me, too.

3 · THE LOST BABIES

BOLINAS LAGOON WAS vast—an expanse of water three and a half miles long, a mile across. Its mouth was formed by a finger-shaped spit of land, Seadrift, emerging from Stinson Beach, and opposite, the shore of Bolinas Beach. The inlet between Seadrift and Bolinas was fast and narrow, less than half a mile wide. At high tide, the ocean rushed into the channel, feeding and filling the lagoon, and at low tide it flowed back out, dropping the lagoon waters. Fishing boats and harbor seals traveled in and out, riding the tides.

Mom and I loved Bolinas Lagoon. She drove around it slowly, so we could watch for animals and birds. During storms and high tides, the water sometimes covered the road. At low tides sandbars appeared in the lagoon, where seals hauled themselves up to sleep and bask in the sun. Along shallow edges great blue herons stood motionless. If we were lucky, we'd see them stalk and then suddenly stab at tiny fish with their long bills. From above, hawks, falcons, osprey, and owls hunted, too. Flocks of black coots traveled the deeper waters, and sometimes the pelicans came. Opposite the lagoon, the snowy egrets nested in the pine trees and, when startled, rose like slow, bright angels.

Our favorite game was to spot the jaunty little blue, black, and white kingfishers, with their crowns of black feathers, who fished from the telephone lines. The first person to spot one shouted, "I see a kingfisher!" On foggy days the lagoon was muted and still, and sometimes it disappeared, with pieces emerging suddenly out of the whiteness. And when the sun broke through, everything came back, the great stretches of water, the birds, the sky.

MOM HAD BAD days. She'd disappear into her bedroom upstairs and we'd go about our lives without her. But on her good mornings, I woke up to her singing along to *Madama Butterfly* or *La Bohème*. Her opera sing-alongs were traditional on Sundays, when she'd also make pancakes. I'd sit at the kitchen table and watch with her while her espresso brewed and the griddle heated up. She'd be dancing around the kitchen in her blue and white flowered kimono, singing, dramatically conducting the opera with a spatula.

She made me special animal-shaped pancakes—rabbits, snakes, dogs, and horses. The horse pancakes were the hardest to flip without breaking off their legs. She used raisins and sunflower seeds for eyes and mouths. If I was quiet and lucky, she'd tell me my favorite story about my dad's bravery.

"Well," she'd begin in her talk-story voice, "during World War II, your father was a merchant seaman and a union shop steward. On one voyage, the captain was a drunk who stayed locked in his cabin. The first mate ran the ship—he carried a gun," my mother whispered.

"And if the men weren't working fast enough, he'd shoot over their heads. One night, in a storm, a barrel of oil broke loose, spilling oil all over the deck. A seaman slipped and broke his leg. A few days later gangrene set in and his leg began to turn green."

My mother's eyes were wide. "But the first mate refused to turn back to port. Your father talked the frightened radioman into sending a secret message, asking for medical advice. The reply said: 'Get that man back to port or he will die.'

"Your father came up with a plan. They staged a fight outside the mate's cabin, and when he came out, they jumped him." Father ran into the cabin to find the gun. But the mate got away, wrestled the gun from Dad, and tried to shoot him. But crewmen jumped the mate again, took the gun, stripped him naked, and handcuffed him to his box spring, a common practice at sea if someone went mad. The first mate was so crazy-strong, he lifted the box spring over his head and chased them.

"Your dad and his men broke into the captain's cabin. The captain was so angry they'd challenged his command that he demanded they all sign a paper, saying they had mutinied, before he would turn the ship around."

Mom paused for effect. "During war, mutiny is punishable by death—but if they didn't sign, the man would die, so they signed. When the ship returned to port, the injured seaman was rushed to the hospital. Your father and his men?" She flicked both her hands. "Poof! They disappeared."

WE HAD BEEN living in our new house for a year when a man came to court my mother. He showed up at our door dressed in a white shirt, his hair slicked back into a ponytail. He carried a bouquet of yellow daises and wild purple irises he picked out on the Mesa.

"Hello, Barbara," he said, holding the flowers out to her. "Remember me? I'm Cliff, I live down the road. I thought you might like these."

Lee leapt up from the dining room table and punched him in the face. Blood spurted all over his shirt.

"Keep your hands off of my mother," Lee said.

"You b'oke my node!" Cliff groaned. Mom burst into tears, and Cliff ran out.

Lee turned to our mother, fists raised. "I won't let you."

She spun away and walked upstairs and into her bedroom, slamming the door.

AMALIA GREW MORE beautiful and sexy. She was playing her flute in chamber music concerts at Marion Wild's house on Horseshoe Hill. Marion Wild had a huge house with many rooms, two Steinway pianos, and a large garden where she held outdoor concerts. She always had two or three musicians living in her place for free, so they could play their music and not have to work. My mother said she was a patron of the arts, like a Medici.

When Amalia played, men flocked to her. They fanned themselves with music programs while her chest rose and fell as she blew into her silver flute. Amalia had a gorgeous, contagious laugh too. Guys followed her everywhere and appeared at all times of night and day. Some were barefoot, with long, wild hair; others came dressed in their best suits. They brought her flowers, bottles of wine, seashells, and polished agates from the beach, sun-bleached bird bones, kittens, poetry written on the backs of old envelopes and sheets of tree bark—anything to try to impress or delight her.

My bedroom window faced the walkway leading to our front deck. When Amalia's boyfriends came visiting, I'd lean out the window and shout, "Hi, you must be Boyfriend Number Five Hundred and Twenty-one."

A guy showed up one night with a guitar slung across his back and carting a ladder. He carried it to the side of the house and climbed up to Amalia's window to serenade her. He tried to get her to climb back down the ladder with him, but she laughingly refused.

Stephen, one of the pianists who lived at Marion Wild's house, asked Amalia out on a date. On a night Mom was out, he came over bringing clams, linguine, wine, and candles, to cook dinner.

"I promise you, this is going to be the best meal you have ever had," Stephen said, fussing with the candles. "I used to be a chef, and you're going to love my food so much you'll marry me."

He sliced the French bread and set it out on the dining room table. We were just sitting down to eat when there were footsteps on the deck. A wild-haired guy strode into the kitchen, bent down, and kissed Amalia fully on the lips. Wordlessly, he lifted her up, slung her over his shoulder, and carried her out the door.

I grinned at Stephen. "Cool," I said. "Are you gonna stay and babysit me?"

My mother bought Amalia macramé halter-tops and velvet miniskirts, encouraging her dating, referring to Amalia's boyfriends as her "suitors."

"Amalia, you're seventeen," Mom told her. "You can do whatever you want, with whomever you want, have fun, but do *not* get pregnant."

One afternoon Amalia rode home in the back of a pickup truck with four men and two other women, to say they were headed across the country to Woodstock, New York, or maybe Canada. My mother wasn't concerned, but I ran after the truck, yelling, "When are you coming back?"

Amalia only laughed and waved. "I'm going on an adventure!"

"Wait!" I screamed. "Wait for me!"

"Don't worry! Becky, I love you! Goodbye!"

She threw back her head and laughed, and the man, sitting next to her, leaned over and kissed her as the truck turned the corner and disappeared. We would not hear from her for a long, long time.

My parents believed that when children ask questions, you should tell them the truth, and usually, my mother did. When I asked her why Amalia and Lee were so much older than me, she told me about the blue babies.

"I lost three babies between you and your sister," she said, "two girls and a boy, all born blue. I think the boy was first—I don't really remember very well—he only lived three days, the second was a girl, and she strangled on her umbilical cord, and the third baby, another girl, was born dead. They didn't live long enough to be named." She smiled sadly at me. "I didn't think I could stand losing another child, but your father really wanted another little girl—and then we had you. The doctors said you might die, too, but you didn't."

"Why did I almost die?" I said.

"Becky, I don't think I want to talk about this any more today, we can talk about it another time." She stood up from the table and smiled at me. "The important thing is that you *lived*."

I was lonesome without Amalia around. I thought about the three blue babies a lot, why I'd lived, why they died instead. I made up names for them: The boy was Michael, and the two girls, Josephine and Kitty. I talked to them under the plum tree, near the creek that ran behind our house. I'd sit down in the patch of blue forget-me-nots under the tree and tell them I was sorry they'd died. I told them I wished they had lived so we could play together.

When I found dead animals and birds on the Mesa—baby quail, mice, voles, shrews, garden snakes—I dug them graves in the field of wild yellow mustard and poison hemlock that grew all around our house. I wrapped each tiny body in toilet paper and buried it. I made crosses out of sticks tied together with weeds and planted one at the head of each grave, ringing each with a circle of pebbles.

Riding home from Ruby's on my bike, I saw a dead mouse in Pat the Bus Driver's driveway. I laid down my bicycle, picked the mouse up, and carried it into his yard. I found a soft spot of dirt and began digging. Pat came out on his porch.

"What are you doing?" he said.

"Burying a mouse," I replied, still digging. "I found it in your driveway."

"Why?"

"Because it's dead. You have to bury things when they die. If you don't, they're sad."

"Makes sense," Pat said. "Can I stay here with you while you work?"

"Okay."

Our cats brought home more dead animals: sparrows and rabbits still warm and half-dead lizards with their tails pulled off. It made me cry. I'd carry their small bodies outside to bury them.

"It's okay," my mother said. "It's natural, they're hunting food for their families, and we're part of their family. They're bringing us gifts."

LEE LEFT. To start an import business, he said. He sent me postcards from Paris, Amsterdam, Bangkok, and Hawaii, all addressed to "My Darling Princess Rebecca." Around the border of each postcard, he drew lines of curving blue waves and little smiling stick men on surfboards.

"The surfing here is magical," he wrote from Hawaii. "The sunsets are fantastic—explosions of pink, orange, and gold. I've been surfing with whales, dolphins, and even sharks. But they don't attack the surfers because there's so many other things for them to eat. Can you believe it? Someday, I will take you to Hawaii, too, and we can swim with the dolphins, together."

He sent small packages filled with sachets of French perfume, sparkly rhinestone clip-on earrings, and gold-colored bracelets. When I played dress-up with my friends, I always had the best stuff to wear.

When Lee was away traveling, my mother and I had quiet nights together. We made popcorn and hot chocolate with rich, Mexican chocolate that my mother grated into steaming milk.

For special occasions, she always made poppy seed cake, allowing me to blend the batter with the electric mixer. Once, the mixer caught my long hair and zoomed up my head, spraying cake batter and bits of hair everywhere. Mom laughed as she untangled me from the mixer, then picked my hair out of the batter, saying, "If you don't tell, no one will ever know."

We played cards, Gin Rummy and Go Fish. Sometimes she played Solitaire and I colored in my coloring books. Mom bought me a set of pens in fifty different colors.

Before coloring, I dumped the pens onto the table and replaced them, one by one, in rainbow order. When I was done, I dumped them out and started again. I began each rainbow with a different shade. Sometimes I started with the blues; others, the reds, or the greens. Sometimes I began with the unusual colors that were hard to fit in, like burnt sienna and umber. I made three or four rainbows before I started coloring. Making rainbows soothed me; a rainbow was beautiful, orderly.

When Lee came home from Colombia, he smuggled in a huge amount of cocaine inside his surfboard. The FBI were waiting for him at the San Francisco Airport, but they couldn't find it. When my mother brought him home from the airport, he was manic, high on the rush of danger. She was infuriated. That night, they had a terrible fight in our kitchen.

"I can't believe you brought that stuff into my house," my mother said.

"How do you think you're going to survive in *your* house without my help?" Lee said.

My mother turned to me. "Becky, go upstairs to your room right now."

I crept up to the top of the stairs, Puppers close on my heels. We sat at the top of the steps, side by side. I wrapped my arms around my dog. She shivered, whined, tried to lick my face.

"You're going to get us all into trouble," my mother said. "I won't have it."

Lee picked up a plate and threw it at my mother. She ducked, and it crashed against the wall.

"Don't you dare throw things at me," she said. "I'm your *mother*." Then she threw a pot at him.

Lee picked up a knife and threw it at the wall. Then he swept a stack of bowls off the shelf onto the floor.

"Stop it, Lee," my mother said.

"Stop it, you guys," I called down to them, clutching Puppers.

"I'll call the cops," my mother said. "Do not make me call the cops."

"You can't call the cops!" Lee said. "Number one rule in this family, right? Isn't that what you and Dad taught me?"

"Get out," my mother said.

Lee threw open the door and stormed out onto the deck. "I'll be back," he yelled. "You cannot just *get rid* of me. You can't."

When I was sure Lee was gone, I crept back down. Puppers trailed behind me. My mother was on her hands and knees, crying and trying to sweep the broken dishes into a grocery bag with her bare hands.

"I don't know what to do," she wept.

My mother let Lee move back into the house, but they continued to fight. When they fought, I stood at the railing at the top of the stairs, Puppers beside me, and dug my thumbnail into the wood.

Twenty-five years after we left that house, I went back and walked through it. I again stood at the top of the stairs and looked down into the living room. I glanced down at my hands on the railing. Beneath my fingers were rows and rows of tiny half-moons gouged into the wood, too many to count. I remembered making those marks. It was *true*, all those terrible fights so long ago. I jerked my hands away.

LEE GOT RICH from that first smuggling venture, and he bought us gifts: a new bike with a banana seat and glittery hand-grips with tassels for me, the ankle-length beaver-skin coat we saved for Amalia, my mother's fur hat.

"Look," Mom said, dancing around in her new hat. "I'm a Russian babushka." She grabbed my hand and dragged me into the living room. She danced me around the couch, doing her best imitation of Tevye from *Fiddler on the Roof.* "If I were a rich man," she sang, "Daidle deedle daidle daidle / Daidle deedle daidle dum / All day long I'd biddy-biddy-bum / If I were a wealthy maaaan . . ."

At Christmastime, Lee tried to fill the house with the magic of Dad. Dad and Lee once had the tradition of illegally topping a tree for our Christmas tree, and Lee wanted to keep this tradition alive. At dusk, he drove Mom's Volkswagen out onto the outer Mesa, where the houses stopped. Mom sat in the front seat, and I rode in back. We drove down a dirt road to the pine tree my brother had picked out earlier in the day. My job was to watch for cops. Lee scaled the tree with a saw and started cutting. When the tree top began to topple, he yelled, "Here it comes!" The tree crashed to the ground, and Lee let out a whoop. Then he raised his saw over his head and shook it against the night sky.

But Lee also grew more and more erratic. From day to day, we didn't know who he would be: the generous son and brother, the surfer calmed by riding waves, or the drugged-out, paranoid smuggler.

One afternoon, my friends Kara and Ruby and I raced down the walkway to the deck. I was way ahead of them and touched the kitchen door to win. I saw Lee inside, stumbling around the kitchen, clad in only a short T-shirt, his dick sticking out, like a pointing red finger, as he swung toward me, his face blind and vacant.

I spun around and shoved Ruby and Kara away from the house.

"Run," I whispered. "Run, run, run."

Lee bought himself a silver Porsche roadster and once talked me into going for a ride in it.

"Where are we going?" I said.

"It's a secret," Lee smiled.

"What kind of secret?"

"It's about your dad, our dad." He glanced at me. "Does Mom ever talk to you about him?"

"Sometimes, but she gets sad if I ask too much."

"I'm going to show you something, okay?"

"Okay."

As we sped over Mount Tamalpais, which separates Bolinas from the rest of the world, my brother lit up a joint.

"How old are you now, Becky?"

"Almost eight."

"But you're smart and you're grown-up for your age, right?"

"Right," I said.

"You have to promise that you will never tell anyone what I'm about to tell you."

"I promise."

"If you ever told anyone, I could be in a whole lot of trouble, and so would you. Do you understand?"

He sucked hard on the joint. I nodded.

"Dad fought very hard so that working men could make a decent wage—he believed all labor was honorable—he did good things, brave things."

I already knew this from Mom, from the stories she told me over and over again. In our family lore, in our stories about ourselves, we're not like other people: We're from the working class, but not of it—we are of the intelligentsia, leaders; we don't need ancestors. We are self-made, wild—phoenixes, every one—creating, burning, re-creating ourselves, my father most of all.

"But those men Dad fought for?" Lee said, "They'll never come out ahead, they're going to work their whole lives, and for what? Nothing. Because the system isn't fair, no matter how hard the unions fight, the rich just get richer and the poor get fucking smashed—but not me. By the time I'm thirty, I'll be rich—I'm gonna make a million dollars. And they're never going to catch me, do you know why?"

"No."

"Because I'm too smart—that's one of the things I got from Dad. Mom's weak, you have to understand that about her."

I stared down at my lap.

"But you're not. You're strong," he said. "Trust me, I just made more money than most people make in their entire lives."

We were on the highway heading north and turned off toward a huge pale yellow building. It sat at the edge of a bay, surrounded by barbed wire fences. Lee parked the Porsche on the side of the road. I could see the dark shape of a guard pacing slowly back and forth in a guard tower.

"Do you know what that is?"

"That's the prison."

"Yeah, San Quentin—do you know who's in there?"

"No."

"The men who murdered our father."

"Oh," I whispered, clenching my hands.

"Those men are in for life. If they ever get released, I'm gonna take care of it, for you, and Amalia and Mom, and for our dad, but you can't ever tell Mom I said that. But don't worry, Becky—I'll always take care of you."

"Can they see us?" I said.

"No," Lee laughed. "They can't, but I'm watching them."

4 · I LOVE YOU, I LOVE YOU

FOR MY EIGHTH birthday, I got two big gifts: a large picture of my father and a fat brown Shetland pony with a white star on her forehead. Her name was Lisa. She cost $35.

My mother built her a corral in our front yard out of thin eucalyptus poles, weaving a gate out of red and green ropes. Then she made a flag—a white unicorn standing against a blue sky—to fly over the enclosure, but Lisa hated her corral. She also hated me.

The second night we had her, she lay down on her side, wiggled out under the fence, and ran away. We brought her back, and my mother added another row of poles to the bottom of the enclosure. Lisa chewed her way through the rope gate and took off again. My mom replaced the rope gate with sliding poles. It didn't matter; the pony still got out.

Every morning, I got up and rushed to the window to see if she'd escaped. If she had, I woke Mother up, got a half bucket of oats, Lisa's bridle, her halter, and her lead rope. My mother grabbed a cup of coffee, and we drove down the dirt roads that crisscrossed the Mesa until we found her.

"Lisa's an escape artist," my mother said.

We usually found her in some weekenders' front lawn, eating rosebuds and grass. Usually these houses were empty, as the owners came to Bolinas only on weekends. We called these people Outsiders. There was an Outsider house up the road from us. We knew when someone was in residence, because there were big, shiny cars parked in the driveway, an American flag hung defiantly in front. The Outsiders did not come into Downtown to shop, but brought their groceries with them. They'd mow their lawns, barbecue chicken and steaks in their backyards. They did not speak to the locals, and we didn't speak to them.

Whenever we passed them on our pony searches, my mother would say "Republicans" under her breath. My pony was eating marigolds one morning in a yard I had never been in before, one filled with white and yellow daisies, blue bachelor's buttons, orange poppies, and lavender bushes. Purple morning glories and white, sweet-smelling jasmine vines climbed all over the trellises out front.

"How beautiful," my mother said. "I wonder who lives here."

I shook the bucket of oats and went after my cranky pony, who had wandered out of sight, beyond the bushy hedge. Mother walked up the stairs to the front porch and knocked. The door opened a crack, and a man with long, stringy hair peered out.

"Hello," my mother smiled. "Sorry to bother you. I've come for my daughter's pony. She's in your garden—she runs away."

"I don't see a pony," he said, "or a daughter." He peered into my mother's face. "Are you a burnout?"

"No, I am not a burnout," my mother said.

"This is a trick, isn't it? It's the unicorn in the garden story, right? Eating the lilies."

"It's not a unicorn, it's a pony."

"That's the trick!" he said and slammed the door.

Lisa grew fat on illicit flowers and hay. Finally, she got so big that she couldn't escape anymore. My mother was worried, and she called the vet.

"I hate to break it to you," the vet said after examining Lisa, "but this pony is not fat—she's pregnant."

"What?"

"Yep, you got two ponies for the price of one."

I knew about pregnant animals. Two of our cats had given birth in my closet. They made nests for their kittens on top of a pile of dirty jeans, underpants, and socks. I sat in the closet watching the kittens nurse, watching their eyes open, and playing with them when they ventured out into the big world of my room.

When the kittens got old enough to give away, my mother dropped me and a box of eleven kittens off in front of the Bolinas Store. On the side of the box she had written FREE TO A GOOD HOME.

"Look sad," she instructed. "You'll get rid of them faster."

"Aren't you going to stay with me?" I said.

"No, people will take pity on a sad-looking little girl with kittens, all by herself. Call me in a couple of hours, and I'll come pick you up. Give away as many as you can."

Most of Saturday, I sat in front of the store, but I gave only three kittens away. My mother herded me and the kittens into the car and drove north to the farmlands outside of Petaluma. We could smell The Cheese Factory several miles before we got there. She pulled the car over to the side of the road. "This is where we leave them," she said.

"They'll die," I cried.

"Don't worry, they'll go to The Cheese Factory and get milk and cheese, and they'll become barn cats and kill lots of mice—they'll be fine. Just take them out of the box, and let's go."

We left them on side of the road. Bewildered, they sat still and watched as we drove away.

"Don't," my mother said. "Do not look back."

JUST AS SHE was about to give birth, Lisa chewed right through the fence and ran away. We drove the whole Mesa, searching and calling, but couldn't find her. Finally, a man who lived on the far side of the Mesa called and said that

Lisa and her newborn colt were hiding in the pasture behind his house.

"I think you better hurry," he said. "She seems nervous, now that she's seen me."

Lisa wouldn't let us near her or her long-legged brown foal. She and the colt slipped through a hole in the fence and trotted away.

Late that night, the man called again. "Your pony's back—you better hurry."

When we got there, the man was in his pajamas, chasing Lisa and her colt around the sides of his swimming pool. Lisa bolted around him, her hooves clattering on the concrete rim. The colt tried to follow but stumbled forward over his own long front legs and fell into the pool. Lisa trotted frantically along the edge, whinnying, as her foal thrashed in the water and began to sink.

"Shit," the man yelled. "Hold on, baby horse! I'm coming."

He jumped into the pool and pulled the thrashing colt into the shallow end, toward my mother's outstretched arms, and together they hauled the colt out of the pool, Mom wrapping the shivering foal in a blanket, then folding him into the backseat of our Volkswagen Bug. I led Lisa alongside the car, and she and her foal nickered back and forth to each other through the open window.

"It's okay," I whispered, patting Lisa's neck as we walked home. "Everything is going to be fine."

We led the ponies down the walkway to the house. I tethered Lisa to the railing, next to the window, where she could see her foal inside the living room. My mother and I dried the colt off and wrapped him in blankets and a heating pad. We made a bed out of sleeping bags and pillows. The colt and I lay down next to the heater.

I looked up at the black-and-white picture of my father, which was *huge*, three feet high and five feet across. In it my father stands next to an old photograph of his hero, Jack London. Jack London's face is smooth and clean, and his hair feathery and light, as if the wind had ruffled it. My father has dark hair and a dark beard and mustache, his eyes alive with presence and humor and shadowed with traces of fatigue, wariness, and some sadness. He is dressed in a shirt and sweater, holding a sheaf of union papers.

As I did whenever I was lonely or scared, I returned to my one perfect memory of my father.

We are in the house on Seventh Avenue in San Francisco. My father is laughing. I run down the hallway, toward the sound, excited. When my father is home, everything is loud and big. The bedroom door is ajar. My father sings. I push the door open. He's wet from the shower, a towel wrapped around his waist and another in his hand. His beard glistens with beads of water. He dances and swirls and snaps the towel at my mother's backside.

"Stop that," she protests. "I'm trying to get dressed." She frowns and pulls a purple slip over her head.

"Didn't you already get enough?" she asks.

"I can never get enough," my father yells happily, whipping the towel off and chasing after her. "I love you, I love you, I love you," he sings as he runs naked across the bedroom and into the sunlight.

I curled up next to the shivering, wet colt, trying to get warm.

The next day, the colt was fine. He ran awkwardly to his mother, and she nickered while she nuzzled him, making sure he was still all there.

THAT HUGE PICTURE of Dad hung around for years. No one ever threw it away, but eventually there was no space big enough for it. It migrated from house to house, from storage unit to storage unit, and finally ended up at my sister's backyard, in an old chicken coop.

She and I felt angry with him one day for choosing his union over us, and we decided to make a ceremony of burning it. I was thirty; Amalia, forty-one. We propped the picture up in a wheelbarrow and doused it with lighter fluid, then said some harsh words to his spirit and lit it. We thought it would go up in a rush of flame, taking our anger with it, but it refused to burn. We poured on more lighter fluid, but it only smoldered; the stench was awful.

After she gave me the picture of Dad, Mom told me more about him. His name was not Dow Wilson. His real name was Rocco Dimimi de Triumveri.

His father was an Italian, from Calabria, in Southern Italy, who left his wife and children there and emigrated to America to make money. He met my grandmother in America and had two children with her.

"Living in *sin*," my mother said.

Dad's father eventually returned to Italy, and my grandmother married a man named Wilson, who became my father's stepfather. Just before World War II broke out, when my father was still a merchant seaman, his ship was going to stop over in Italy, so he wrote to his father and asked to meet him.

But when they docked, Dad was embarrassed, and he waited until all the other crewmen were off the ship before setting out to find his father.

One of the sailors came back onboard before he could and said, "Hey, Dow. You know anyone on board named Rocco? There's some crazy little Italian man down on the dock asking for Rocco."

"No," my father lied.

But my father did go find his father sitting on the edge of the pier. The man was clutching a gift, a bottle of olive oil, crying, "Rocco, *mio figlio*, my son." They spent one day together. They never saw each other again.

Grandfather and Grandmother Wilson lived in Arizona, but my mother had not seen them since my father died. I had met them only once, when I was a baby. We had one picture of them, a paunchy man with his arm around a thin, gray-looking woman with a pointy chin, neither of them smiling.

She told me Grandfather Wilson hated Italians and beat my father with a belt. When dad was eight years old, he went to school and wrote his name at the top of his paper, *Rocco de Triumveri*. The teacher asked him to come up to the blackboard and write his name again. He did. The teacher crossed it out, wrote *Dow Wilson*, and said, "This is your name now."

Dad ran away from home at fourteen. His first job was working for a door-to-door salesman who sold his wares to lonely women and traded for sex when they could not pay. When he was fifteen, my father went into the merchant marine.

I learned my father's real name when I was nine, and I told my mother, "I'm going to be Italian like my dad," and I began writing *Becky di Triumveri* at the top of my papers at school. When teachers called me Becky Wilson, I refused to answer.

Once a year, mother and I made the trip to Auburn, California, near Sacramento, to visit her parents, but never stayed overnight. She said they were deeply unhappy, had been for years. As a young man, her handsome father, Ron, tried to be a movie star, but failed, and instead, he became a door-to-door brush salesman, with a string of lovers. Her mother, Betty, found his collection of love letters and punished him by "making his life *miserable*."

It was a ritual on the long drive up for my mother to tell me how her parents had disowned her when she married my father.

Each time, as was expected of me, I asked, "Why?"

"Because your father was a communist," she replied. "But then, so was I."

"Tell me again how you met him," I begged. "That's the best part."

They'd met in San Diego, during a labor strike. My mother was working the switchboard for the International Longshoremen and Warehousemen Union. "I took it *so* seriously. I thought I was very important," she said.

After an evening union meeting, Mother was typing away and my father came up to her desk and started flirting. His friend Jerry was high on marijuana and couldn't stop giggling. He kept falling over, and Dad had to prop him up against the wall repeatedly. My mother tried to ignore them, but finally she got mad and told them to get the hell out of her office.

"Two weeks later, we got married," she smiled. "I didn't really want to, but your father was insistent."

When she took him to meet her parents, they all argued. My father left and swore he wouldn't set foot in his in-laws' home again. Whenever they went to visit after that, my mother carried meals out to my father, who sat on the hood of the car while everyone else ate inside.

"My mother only stood up for me once in my whole life," Mom said, looking grim.

When war started, Mother was eighteen. She moved to San Diego and became a production worker like "Rosie the Riveter," drafting blueprints for bombers and fighter planes.

She got pregnant by another man. Abortions were illegal.

"You had to find someone, who knew someone, who knew a doctor, who would give you an abortion," she explained.

After the abortion, she developed an infection but couldn't go to a doctor or to a hospital. She nearly died.

"I didn't know who else to call, so I called my mother, and she came. She lied to my father about where she was—she took care of me until I got well." My mother fell silent. "That's it," she said finally, thumping the steering wheel. "Once, in my whole life."

"Didn't she love you?" I asked.

My mother smiled ahead at the road. "The truth is, I have no idea."

I THOUGHT ONCE that I could please my mother by cleaning her bathroom. I hung up all the towels and emptied the trash can, wiped off the American flag toilet lid, straightened all of her lotions, her hairspray cans, her jar of Dippity-do hair gel, her perfumes. I put them into neat rows according to size, their labels facing out, and stood her lipsticks up.

"Look," I said proudly, when she came home.

My mother took one look and swept everything onto the floor.

"I *hate* straight lines," she said. "They remind me of my mother."

Her parents, the Goulds, lived in a two-story Victorian outside of Auburn. They never seemed to remember how old I was. At Christmas and on my birthday, they regularly sent me packets of floral underwear that were consistently too big, the waistband reaching my armpits. But as we drove down the dirt road on the way to their house, I always got excited. Each time I thought it would be different. Fun. Maybe they would give me a present.

But each visit was the same. Grandma in the house cooking, Grandpa out in the garage, surrounded by his pack of semiwild cats. When we got out of the car, he and the half-feral cats simply watched.

Grandpa would nod a curt hello and say, "I'll take Becky down to the canal and show her the water."

He'd lead me down the path toward the huge aqueducts that pumped water through the Central Valley. Then he'd grab me by the neck and force me to look down into the water rushing through the concrete channel.

"Do you see that?" he'd yell over the roar of the water.

"Yes, Grandpa," I'd say.

"You are never to come here alone," he'd say, shaking me hard. "You can get killed if you fall in," he hissed in my ear. "A little boy fell in and drowned. You stay away from this water."

Their living room had thick brown wall-to-wall carpeting. I was not allowed in there either, not since the trip Grandma caught me drawing shapes with my fingers in the pile of the carpet. Neither was I was allowed to touch her china. At lunch, I had to sit by myself at a card table, covered with a plastic tablecloth, eating off a plastic plate with plastic utensils.

After lunch, Grandpa went back to his shed and Grandma showed me the family quilts. She kept them carefully preserved in tissue paper and stashed under the guest beds we were never invited to sleep in. She'd unwrap the quilts one by one and say, "You'll get these when I die, but only if you're *good*." She always smelled of White Shoulders perfume, and under that, faintly of alcohol.

On our last trip to their house, I said, "Why can't I have them now? Why do I have to wait until you're dead?"

My grandmother recoiled and narrowed her eyes at me. "How dare you speak to me like that?"

I stuck my chin out at her. "Fucker," I said.

She grabbed me by the hair. "I'm going to wash your mouth out with soap, just like I did to your mother when she talked back to me."

I hollered and tried to kick her in the shins, but she pulled me into the bathroom and locked the door. She turned on the tap and grabbed the soap. She shoved the bar into my mouth and ground it into my teeth. "This will wash that foul language out of your mouth."

I heard Mom outside the door, crying and calling, "Don't, please don't."

After that terrible trip, my mother decided things might go better if Grandma and Grandpa came to our house instead of us going to theirs. The morning of their first visit, Mom and Lee argued about Grandma and Grandpa. Lee and his current girlfriend, Kathy, were in the kitchen making vegetarian pizza.

"We've gotta get out of here before they get here," Lee said to Kathy.

"You have to stay," my mother pleaded. "You have to give me moral support."

"Oh, no," Lee said. "I hate that old witch—you're on your own."

Mother turned on me and said, "Rebecca di Triumveri, or whatever the hell your name is these days, get upstairs and clean your room before your grandparents get here."

I was stuffing my toys and dirty clothes into the closet when I heard Lee say, "Oh, shit, they're here."

I ran to the window. Grandma and Grandpa's brown El Dorado was just pulling up. I ran down the stairs chanting, "They're here, they're here."

"Run," Lee said to Kathy. "Out the back door." And I raced after them.

"Goddammit, Lee," Mom called after him. "You get back here and help me."

Lee vaulted over the railing and landed in the bushes below the deck. "Get the pizza," he called.

Kathy ran back into the house, grabbed the pizza, and raced back out.

"Throw it," my brother shouted. Kathy swung her arm back and tossed the pizza off the deck. Lee leapt up and caught it with both hands.

"Jump," he said. Kathy swung her legs over the railing and leapt. I was halfway over the railing when my mother grabbed the back of my pants.

"Oh, no you don't, missy—*you* are staying here with *me*."

When Grandma Betty died many years later, gin bottles were found stashed throughout her house, in closets, under sinks, in her extra purses, enough to fill six Hefty trash bags. At her memorial, the pastor said, "Betty Gould was a champion rose gardener, she was also known for her sharp tongue."

Amalia and I looked at each other and burst out laughing.

5 · REGULAR THINGS

AMALIA NEVER MADE it to Woodstock; she went back to Echo Park. She called Mom from a pay phone to say she was with Luis, now her boyfriend, and she was pregnant.

"And guess what, Mom?" Amalia said. "We're getting married in a Catholic church."

There was a loud crash in the bathroom.

"Amalia, can you hold on?" My mother opened the bathroom door. Dad's decoy ducks had fallen off the wall onto the floor. We could read the white letters carefully stenciled on the bottom of each duck: *D Wilson*. Mother returned to the phone.

"Amalia? I don't know what to say except I think you're too young, but you're eighteen, and it's your life. Somehow, I don't think your father would approve of you getting married in a Catholic church."

"Okay, maybe not the church," Amalia conceded. "But Mom, I'm in love."

Later, Mom told the story about the decoys falling over and over. "He spoke from the *Other Side*," she laughed.

But at home she was angry. She told me she'd wanted Amalia to marry a rich man who would take care of her and let her play her music.

Still, she prepared for Amalia's baby. She designed a birth announcement to give to her friends, scowling as she worked: a silkscreen image of a very pregnant, naked woman with one hand on her belly. Behind her stood a man holding an umbrella over her. Raindrops splashed against the top of the umbrella. IT'S A BABY! read the caption. COME CELEBRATE!

Before flying down to L.A. to see Amalia and meet our future in-laws, Mother planned a shopping trip to San Francisco. Going to the City with her made me anxious, as the City reminded her of Dad. Sometimes, she was fine, and would tell me about Dad, but other times, she would pull over to the side of the road and weep. I learned to sit quietly while she cried. If I tried to comfort her, she'd only weep harder.

"This trip will be fun, Becky," my mother said. "We're going to Macy's, and Magnin is having a sale."

When we crossed the Golden Gate Bridge toward San Francisco, my mother told me how my father was responsible for the first black painters to work on the bridge, my dad's union being one of the first unions on the West Coast to integrate. When Dr. Martin Luther King, Jr. marched on Washington, D.C., Dad organized a parallel civil rights demonstration in San Francisco. He also supported César Chávez's Farm Workers Union—when he went to meet with César Chávez, he brought soccer balls for the kids. I felt proud of my dad every time we crossed the bridge, as if it were a little bit mine.

Crossing this same bridge going home to Bolinas, she'd talk of his longshoreman days, before the painters' union. We looked north across the Bay to Point Richmond, where his ships departed from. We could also see the hulking shape of San Quentin prison to the west, where my father's killers were imprisoned. I looked for the large carrier ships moving slowly past Alcatraz Island and passing under the bridge. I imagined my father on such a ship, waving to my mother on the shore as he sailed out to sea.

I didn't know it then, but my brother smuggled huge shipments of marijuana into the Port of San Francisco inside some of those carrier vessels, with the help of partners, some of them from our father's longshoreman days.

They were rough men, these men my father and brother worked with. Lee once threatened to kill his partners and woke up naked under the front wheel of a truck, his ankles and wrists bound with duct tape, his mouth taped shut, as a warning.

In those days, he had trash bags full of money. Once Lee drove his Porsche to a friend's house. He was frantic, certain the cops were following him, and he'd zigzagged across the Mesa, trying to lose them. He arrived with cocaine spilled down the front of his pants and begged a pair of scissors with which he cut his trouser legs off so the cops would not find coke on his clothes. But the cops were not after him; he was just having a bad, bad trip.

WHEN WE DROVE through the City, Mom pointed out the streets, and sometimes the houses, where my family had lived. She told me how my father turned the hose on the landlady on rent day when he did not have the rent money, and how on Christmas Eve, my parents shopped for bargains at the midnight sale at Macy's. I always asked, "Did I live there, too?" and the answer was always, "No, that was before you were born."

But we did not go the house where we all lived when Dad was shot, and we did not go to the Mission District, where Dad worked, where he'd died on the street, on South Van Ness.

We started our shopping day at Macy's department store at Union Square. I loved the cable cars, the street performers, and inside Macy's, the mirrors and fancy makeup displays, and the elegant, bejeweled saleswomen. My mother became her haughty self, taking her time over the lipsticks and polishes. She never wore any makeup except lipstick—the color had to be exactly right. She had long, beautiful feet, and she liked to show them off in sandals, her toenails painted blue with a layer of silver glitter. She didn't paint her fingernails, because she thought it impractical and vain.

At Magnin, Mom tried on dresses and finally emerged from the dressing room tall and regal in a white caftan with a large blue paisley pattern and bell sleeves. She also bought a wig wrapped in nylon mesh, and a small brown bun to pin at the nape of her neck. The wig came with a round pink carrying case that looked just like a plastic purse. She christened the dress and the wig her "mother-in-law outfit."

"This makes me look more respectable," she said, pinning the wig on. She surveyed herself in the mirror and smoothed the front of her new dress.

"It doesn't match," I said. "Your hair has a lot of gray in it."

My mother glared at me. "Who asked you?"

She wore her new mother-in-law outfit to a party at Eugene's house. Eugene and his wife were old union friends. The party was crowded; I took off to find Eugene's daughter, Eileen. It was 1970, and she was eleven, three years older than me, but not very smart.

"We can play Horror of Dracula upstairs," I said. "I'll be Count Dracula and Jonathan Harker, the vampire slayer, and you can be Lucy."

We dressed Eileen up in her mother's nightgown and used her mother's lipstick. We were acting the scene where Dracula bites Lucy's neck when Eugene came in.

"Hello, girls." he said. "Oh, don't you look grown-up."

He closed the door and sat down on the edge of the bed. "Becky, come sit on my lap and give me a kiss."

"No," I said.

"Eileen likes to sit on my lap," he said.

Eileen began to cry.

"No," I said.

"Come on, Becky," he said. "Sit right here."

"No," I said, and turned to Eileen. "Go get a rope, we're gonna tie him up."

Eileen came back with two extension cords. "It's all I could find," she said.

I pulled on Eugene's arm. "Go sit on the chair."

"Is this a new game?" he asked, swaying.

"Yeah," I said. Eileen and I tied him to the chair with one extension cord and tied his ankles together with the other.

"Okay, girls," he said. "You've got me now."

He tried to kiss us as we danced by. My mother opened the bedroom door and stared at us open-mouthed.

Eugene said, "Barbara, these girls have got me all tied up."

She grabbed me by the ear and marched me out of the house to our car.

"Get in," she said, baring her teeth at me. "Right now."

"Mom, he tried to kiss me."

"That's enough," she said.

"He tried to make us sit on his—"

"Eugene worked for your father—what were you thinking? You embarrassed me."

I HAD LEARNED about Dracula at school when our teachers decided we were old enough to choose our own films. We chose *The Curse of Frankenstein* and *Horror of Dracula*. I wanted to be Lucy, Dracula's favorite victim. She wore filmy white dresses and a small golden cross around her white neck.

At home I traipsed around my room in the white nylon nightie I'd bought at a rummage sale that I hid from my mom under my bed.

Our teachers suddenly canceled our film privileges. There had been an accident. Kenny, a first grader, had been playing Dracula in his parents' garage and had splashed gasoline over his own head and lit a match: trying to kill Dracula. He survived, but with second- and third-degree burns all over his body. When he recovered enough, he and his family left town.

I then became afraid of Dracula and placed little rows of garlic along each windowsill in my bedroom. I traded a plastic horse for a fake silver cross and stuffed the white nightie at the bottom of the trash can.

I was in the third grade that year. There was a new girl in our class named Jill. My mother was on a health food kick, so I got raw pumpkin and sunflower seeds and apples in my lunch bags, or a can of tuna and a can opener, if she'd forgotten to go shopping. But Jill's mother made peanut butter and jelly sandwiches on Wonder bread for her and her brother, so we swapped. I liked going to Jill's house and always worked my way around to asking for white bread. I loved mashing it into a ball and stuffing it in my mouth.

"Why do you like Jill so much?" my mother asked. "Her family's *straight*."

"I like her," I said. "She's nice."

Jill's family invited me to go to church with them. Jill and I went to Bible school. We received booklets about being good Christians, and I snuck them home. I liked a picture of a blue-robed Jesus blessing beautiful Mary Magdalene, all of which I needed to keep secret from my mother—she would be displeased. My mother liked to say, quoting Karl Marx, "Religion is the opiate of the people."

Somehow, my mother knew: "This church thing is just a phase for you," she said, with her arms crossed. "But I sure hope it passes soon."

At Sunday school, I made her a cross. On a small square of wood, I carefully traced the shape of a cross and then glued colored rocks all over it. Triumphant, I brought it home to her.

"Mom, look what I made for you."

She took it outside and tossed it off the deck, saying, "No crosses in *my* house."

IRONICALLY, MY MOTHER went back to school to get a teaching credential in special education at Dominican College, the Catholic school founded and run by the Dominican Sisters of San Rafael. She wanted to teach autistic and handicapped children—I wasn't allowed to call them "retarded." She went to work building huge, boxlike structures with switches, flashing lights, and buttons that triggered loud sounds and bird whistles, these to stimulate responses from children who did not know how to connect with the world as a normal child would—hence, she called these *learning environments*. In researching her environments, we went to the San Francisco Exploratorium and went through the Tactile Dome, a dark maze we found our way through by touch. At the end, we slid down into a room filled with birdseed. Evenings and weekends she went to class.

"You're nine, you're old enough to take care of yourself," she said. But I got into trouble. I fell while playing with Ruby on our deck and split the side of my face open. Ruby got her dad, who was a doctor. I thought a kind doctor dad would be the best dad to have, a dad who could always fix you. But Ruby's dad was exploring alternative medicines, especially the power of the mind, and marijuana, so he wouldn't stitch the cut. Instead he told me to imagine myself surrounded with white light. Ruby was mortified, and she and her mom stuck Band-Aids over my wound. When Mom got home, she rushed me to the ER, where the doctor sewed twenty-seven stitches in my head.

I have a school class photo from that time. My hair is in two long ponytails and I'm sitting up straight, smiling eagerly. I have my father's blue eyes, his mouth, and my own crooked teeth. I'm wearing a white dress with rows of pink hearts. My turquoise tights are torn at the left knee. My black shoes have purple velvet bows that my mother made because I'd worn the old laces out. My right arm is in a plaster cast.

Mom hired a live-in babysitter for me, but had to fire him after he led me and his son on a parade across the Mesa holding a burning cross. Mom then explained to me the terrible symbolism of burning crosses, the terrorizing of black and Jewish people. Ruby's family was Jewish, and I was deeply ashamed. I begged Mom not to tell Hannah, Ruby's mom.

Mom never told Hannah on me—I was thirty-three years old before I ever told that story. Hannah and I went out to dinner, and then we sat up late, drinking tea and talking about those days in Bolinas, and I confessed.

Hannah listened kindly, and then she said, "I talked to your mother about leaving you alone so much. I told her kids need things to be regular—they like regular meals at regular times—but your mother shook her head and said, 'No, Hannah, I don't want Becky to be dependent, I want her to be strong.'"

MOM FINISHED HER first year of school at Dominican College. She'd arranged for us to swap houses with the

Moores, a family of artists who lived just outside Bozeman, Montana, for our summer vacation. The house came with two horses.

Kara came with us—we took nearly a week driving there. When we arrived the first thing we did was run to see the horses in the pasture beside the house. Both were mares, one a buckskin with a black stripe running down her back, the other a bay.

"They look kinda big," whispered Kara, nervously.

"We already know how to ride," I reminded her.

"Yeah, but we ride ponies, Becky," Kara said.

"So what?" I told her. "I'm not scared."

The note left on the kitchen table said the mares' names were Moccasin and Shaheia. The note also said that Nancy, from the neighboring ranch, would come over and show us how to care for them.

Mom had bought me a cowboy hat, pink felt, with a thin pink satin ribbon hat band and a wide, flat brim. It made me look like Dale Evans, she said. But in Montana, the cowboys and cowgirls we saw wore only white straw or black felt hats, so people turned to look at me. I stuffed it under the backseat of the car.

"I look stupid," I told my mom.

"What's wrong with being different?" my mother said.

She also tried to buy us hard hats at the local saddle shop.

"You mean those yellow things construction workers wear?" the clerk said.

"No, the black ones, the kind that English horse riders wear—for the girls, in case they fall off."

"English riders? *Shee-et*, lady," the man said. "This is Montana—we don't wear *hard hats*."

Nancy was eighteen and had a long, blond ponytail. She wore skintight jeans and hand-tooled black cowboy boots. Nobody in Bolinas dressed like her. Nancy chewed and snapped her gum while she talked, telling us all about the horses. Moccasin was a purebred twenty-year-old quarter horse who'd been bred with an Arabian to get Shaheia—her name was a Blackfoot Indian one; Nancy didn't know what it meant. Shaheia was ten. When she was a foal, she had gotten tangled in barbed wire and torn her chest badly. The vet who treated her beat her when she wouldn't stand still for him to stitch her up.

"That damned vet made a man-hater out of that mare," Nancy said and spat. "Whenever a man's near her, she shows the whites of her eyes."

She continued with our instructions. "Now, when you're cinching them up, you gotta check for bloating," she said.

"What's that?" I asked.

"Some horses hate the feeling of being tightly cinched into saddles, so they suck air into their bellies on purpose and hold it—that's bloating. Then, after you've cinched 'em up, they let the air out, and your girth is too loose, and your saddle will slip. You really gotta watch Shaheia, she *loves* to bloat. See how tight this girth is now? Try to get your fingers under it."

I tried but couldn't.

"Well, watch this—this is how you get them to stop bloating." Nancy kneed Shaheia sharply in the belly. Shaheia grunted, blew her air out. Nancy quickly yanked on the girth strap, cinched it up another few inches, looping and knotting it tight.

"You see that?" she asked. "Gotta check them every time."

The next morning, I said to Kara, "Let's get the horses saddled up and go for a ride before Nancy gets here."

"Your mom said we had to wait for Nancy." My mother was in the kitchen making coffee.

"We don't have to tell her," I said. "Don't be a chicken."

We caught the horses and quickly saddled them up. "Just wait until Nancy sees us," I said.

The horses were so tall we couldn't get on by ourselves and we needed to climb up on the corral fence to be able to reach the stirrups. Once we mounted, we trotted slowly up and down the trail a few times, waiting for Nancy, and then we got bored.

"Let's wave at my mom," I said.

She was sitting in the window seat that faced the creek, working on a knitting project. The winter before, she'd started making what she called *wearable art*. She began with a sewing project, making me a miniskirt out of layers of scalloped pieces of suede that looked like fish scales, but she'd forgotten to put a zipper in the back, so I couldn't put it on.

"Oh, well," she said, "Maybe a wall hanging?"

In Montana, she moved from sewing to knitting and was working on a women's unity skirt. It was a long, curling piece, blue and green, picturing big-breasted women of all colors holding hands. Their hair streamed behind them like strands of seaweed in gold, green, and orange.

"Let's show her how good we are," I said as I reined Shaheia around.

"HEEEYAH!" we shouted as we kicked the horses' flanks. They broke into a lope. We swung around the side of the house and kicked again to make them go faster.

As we raced past the house, Shaheia's saddle slid to the side, and I slid with it. I tried to hold on to her mane, but the saddle kept sliding until it was under her belly, where I hung upside down. Shaheia galloped right past the window where my mother was sitting, then she bucked, and I fell to the ground. Shaheia jumped me and galloped off, bucking and kicking, dragging her saddle.

Kara reined up beside me.

"Shit!" I spat out dirt. My mother was still sitting in the window, knitting, head down—she hadn't even noticed. I whispered to Kara, "We gotta catch Shaheia and put her back, hurry!"

We caught her and snuck both horses around the back of the house, took off their tack, rubbed them down with handfuls of straw, and turned them back out to the pasture. I washed myself up in the water trough.

"What if your mom saw?" Kara said. "She'd never let us ride again."

"She didn't, and don't tell," I said.

When Nancy finally came, she found us sitting up on the fence like good girls, waving.

THERE WAS A stream behind the house. It was small, but seemed to have the force of a river, with fast, clear water shooting over big, smooth rocks. From our beds, we could hear rapids at night, after my mother turned off her music. The water was too fast and too cold to swim in. Mother said it could carry you downstream, all the way to Bozeman, but not until it had frozen you into a giant girl-size ice cube.

But on the hottest days, she tied one end of a rope around a tree, and Kara and I took turns tying the other end around our waists and leaping into the rushing water. Instantly, the icy water sucked us under, froze our hands and feet, and shot us downstream until we reached the end of the rope, water beating against our heads as we screamed for my mother to save us. She pretended not to hear and sat reading under the tree. Eventually, she laid her book down, got up, and dragged us out, and we crawled, blue-lipped and grinning, onto the stream bank and into the sun.

When we returned to Bolinas, I didn't want my pony anymore. She had run away, thrown me, scraped me off her back by running under low tree branches, kicked me, and bitten me too many times, so I now disliked her as much as she hated me. I was ruined for ponies: Now I wanted a *real horse*, like Shaheia.

"Why don't you call the Moores, ask them if they want to sell her," my mother suggested. "They don't ride her, and their kids are all in college."

I called them and they said yes, they'd sell her to me for $150. My mother arranged for Shaheia to be trucked down to California in the spring. Meanwhile, I sold hateful Lisa and her foal to the local farrier, or horseshoer, who came every few months to trim the ponies' hooves.

Shaheia arrived six months later, showing up in early May. She snorted, reared, and rolled her eyes as they backed her out of the trailer. I held my breath: She was tall and beautiful and *mine*.

We boarded my horse in a pasture by the side of the main road leading into town, a two-mile walk from our house. After school, I'd sling a halter, lead rope, and bridle over my shoulder, and Puppers and I would head off across the Mesa and down the hill. I'd climb on top of a car or a fence and jump on Shaheia and ride her bareback. Her back was wide and long, and I could lie back with my arms open, rocking side to side as she walked. Sometimes I rode with other girls, but usually I rode alone.

I rode when my mother was depressed or my brother was raging. The three of us—me, my dog, and my horse—would roam the hills surrounding Bolinas, or gallop on the beach. We'd race, me leaning forward alongside Shaheia's neck, gripping with my legs, until her neck and flanks were foamy and dark with sweat, then we'd walk to cool down. I'd sing to her and to Puppers, sing to Dad, too.

Sometimes, I rode down the beach to the mouth of the lagoon, and if the tide was at its lowest, I'd swim Shaheia across the channel from Bolinas to Seadrift. This was dangerous—if the tide was going out too fast, or if you didn't enter the water far enough inland, you could get swept out to sea. I'd cling to Shaheia as she surged beneath me, fighting against the tide, her black tail streaming in the water, Puppers swimming behind us. Touching land on the other side, she'd grunt and shake her whole body, nearly shaking me off. Then I'd slide off her wet back so she could roll in the sand.

I loved her big firm belly, the smell of her horsey sweat, the feel of her soft nose, her breath on my hands. Shaheia meant freedom to me. She was magic. In the summer, when the white fog rolled in off the ocean and over us as we rode, I'd hold on to Shaheia's black mane with both hands, lean into her neck, close my eyes, and let her find the way back home.

6 · HERO

M Y MOTHER HAD told me my father was killed by robbers, so when I first learned the truth of my dad's murder, it was by accident.

I found the newspaper clippings in a wooden box in the living room. It had a dull brass plaque with my father's initials, DW, etched into the lid. The box had sat there for years. My mother told me it contained personal papers. One day when I was nine, I opened it.

The box is filled with old, yellowed newspapers. They feel dry and stiff in my hands, hard to unbend. The one on top shows a graphic black-and-white drawing of a hand holding a smoking shotgun, white fingers curled around the pump. Beneath the shotgun, a man lies on his back, his arms out and one leg bent at the knee, the other, lying straight out on the pavement, blood pooled around the body. The white, hand-lettered writing inside the black smoke curling out of the shotgun reads, WHOSE HANDS PAID FOR THIS?

In English and Spanish, the text reads: "$30,000 reward for information leading to the arrest and conviction of the murderer of San Francisco Painters Union Officer Dow Wilson, shot at 1 AM, April 5, 1966. Contact the San Francisco Police or your local FBI office."

My heart pounds. "Mom," I call out. "What is this?"

She comes into the living room, drying her hands on a dishtowel. When she sees the open box, she stops stock-still. "Oh," she says. "You found them."

"What is all this?" I ask again.

"They're articles about your father's murder."

"I thought he was killed by robbers."

My mother sighs deeply. "Well, in a way, he was. A union man stumbled on evidence that a union official named Rasnick was stealing money from the union, *a lot of money*. He brought the information to your father, and he and a small group of men decided to bring this man, Rasnick, down—but Rasnick found out. He had your father killed. That's kind of like robbers, isn't it?"

I look down at the drawing of my father I'm holding. My hands start to shake, my chest constricts, I can't move.

"Becky, please put those away. We'll go through them another time. I was planning to take you to where his ashes are buried this year, and next month is the anniversary of his death—let's talk about it then."

She takes the clippings from my hands, puts them back in the box, shuts the lid.

Later that night, after my mother is in bed, I sneak down to the living room, quietly open the old wooden box, take out the clippings, and read about my father's murder. There are articles from the *San Francisco Chronicle*, the *Washington Post*, *Time* magazine, *Newsweek*, and the *Bay Area Painters News*. One paper wrote,

DEATH OF A WILD MAN

Wilson, a swashbuckling, Shakespeare spouting romantic

was also a volatile, foulmouthed labor leader

he called the International officials, "high-class pimps"

he commanded the unwavering allegiance of nearly all 2,600 local members

was famous for his casual dress of jeans and sweater

wore a beard and mustache like Fidel Castro . . .

Local No.4 called his murder a political assassination and offered a reward of $27,000 for information leading to the killers. On April 7, two days after his murder, the California State Assembly held its "First Extraordinary Session" and wrote a resolution memorializing him, lauding him for leading a union "whose membership was the most fully integrated in the nation," noting the first black painters working on the Golden Gate Bridge, and my father's commitment to civil rights. "He could mingle with any group without giving or asking anything more than equality, a leader whose integrity and principles engendered love in many and hatred in a misguided few . . ."

Night after night, I creep down the stairs in my nightgown, careful to step on the outsides of the staircase so the steps don't squeak. I read hungrily about my father, my family.

Two thousand people attended the memorial for my father at the Labor Temple. Congressman Philip Burton wept as he gave the eulogy; they all sang "We Shall Overcome."

I read in one interview with my mom that in our old neighborhood my father had organized two teenage basketball teams and called them "The Black Bastards" and "The Irish Bigots." He always played on the side of The Black Bastards, she said.

I read a speech she'd made:

During most of my husband's tempestuous life, I stayed in a somewhat protected backwater, enjoying vicariously his many triumphs, his few defeats. The window I had into Dow's life was so fascinating, the show so dramatic, that I could not resist. His joy of living was so great that it infected all of us with a kind of excitement for ideas, controversy, fun, love, anger. The whole gamut of human emotions ran wild through our household, up and down the hallways, with everyone trying to upstage Dad.

The *Chronicle* followed the murder investigation, the case breaking when a man named Wally Charleston contacted the San Francisco police, saying he'd been offered $5,000 to kill my father the February before.

"I was introduced to a big guy with hard eyes," he said, who handed him an envelope with a $2,500 advance to "dump" a guy from Local No. 4 in Oakland whose last name began with a *D*. "My blood ran cold when I heard that," Charleston said. "I gave it back and told him I was checking out."

He went to the police only to be told there was no union official in Oakland whose last name began with *D* and that Local No. 4 was in *San Francisco*. Charleston decided he had been conned. After my father was shot, Charleston contacted the police again and told them it was my father he had been approached to kill. His mistake had been that he thought "Dow Wilson" was all one name.

"God, if I'd tried harder in February," Charleston said. "He was a family man." He agreed to go undercover and wear a wire.

In May, a second union official, Lloyd Green, the financial secretary of the Hayward Painters Union, was shot and killed. Like my father, he fought against corruption in the union leadership. Union members all over the Bay Area staged demonstrations in front of the homes of the Mayor of San Francisco and the local U.S. Attorney General. The reward to help catch the murderers grew to $42,275.

Charleston continued to work undercover, leading the police first to Carl Black, the accountant for Local 478 in Sacramento; then to the driver, Norman Call, the man with hard eyes; and the hit man, Max Ward. Call and Ward were both members of Local 478's welfare fund. The police investigation then led them to Rasnick, Financial Secretary for District Council 16—the mastermind.

Rasnick, Call, and Ward were all indicted, each tried separately. They were represented by the theatrical and famous criminal defense attorney Melvin Belli. The *Chronicle* called Ward's trial a "Tale of Brutality." The prosecution revealed that $100,500 had been stolen from Sacramento Local 478's Welfare Fund and argued that if the audit my father called for had been conducted, Ward, Rasnick, and Call would have been charged with embezzlement. Call was tried and found guilty of first-degree murder. He then confessed, saying Rasnick ordered the killings of Wilson and Green to stop their "agitation" against "higher-ups" in the union.

Ward was also convicted. My brother—then eighteen—attacked him right in the courtroom, punched him in the face. "I don't blame him," Ward told the reporters.

In Rasnick's trial, the prosecution read aloud from his police interrogation. Of my father, Rasnick said, "The guy was a commie, and a beatnik and a bum, garbage . . ."

Rasnick's was declared a mistrial, but—later that year—he was tried for and convicted of Green's murder. Allegations about orders from "higher-ups" were never proven. All three were sent to San Quentin for life.

Photographs accompanied the stories: my mother, looking sad, shaking the hand of San Francisco Mayor John F. Shelley, who was promising to bring the killers to justice. My brother in the courtroom, held down by two men after hitting the killer. Fourteen-year-old Amalia on a picket line carrying a sign that read NO MORE ORPHANS! Me: a toddler, playing in a sandbox in the park.

I stare at the flat gray and black faces of the killers until I feel sick, their names rolling around in my head like marbles.

"WHERE IS IT?" I asked my mother as we got into the car. I had picked a bouquet of wild irises and daffodils to take to his grave.

"Near the overlook above Muir Beach."

My mother tried to get me to sing rounds with her as we drove, but I refused. I pushed my feet against the floor of the car, wanting it to go faster. Finally, we got there. I climbed out of the Bug and looked around. A railed path zigzagged down along the point and ended where the cliff dropped into the sea. Across the water to the left, San Francisco was wreathed in fog; to the right, there was the open ocean. Sage, coyote bush, paintbrush, and bright, purple lupine covered the point below us.

I turned to my mother. "Where is he?"

My mother bit her bottom lip and glanced around. "I don't know. Somewhere around here."

"You don't *know*? What do you mean you don't know?"

"He said he left a marker . . ."

"Who? Who said?"

"Gordon, a friend of your father's. He buried the ashes, said he left a plaque above them."

"There isn't a *gravestone*?"

My mother began to cry. "It was dark. We stole his ashes from the mortuary—I didn't want anyone to know where we were taking him. I made Gordon bring the ashes up here and bury them in the middle of the night." She wept. "I wanted him," she said. "And I didn't want the union to have him."

I dropped my flowers and climbed over the railing.

"Where are you going?" my mother said. "Stop."

I pulled furiously at a bush. "To find my dad," I said. Sobbing, I uprooted a coyote bush and began to beat the ground with it.

"Becky. Please listen to me. They wanted to build a memorial to him in Golden Gate Park. They wanted to make him a hero."

"He was a hero," I said. *"My father was a hero.* I know. I read the newspapers, I read it in the newspapers and magazines you hid."

"I was going to show you," she wept.

"When?"

"When you were older."

I flung the bush at her. "He was *my father*," I said. *"Mine."*

My mother opened her arms and pleaded. "Please, I'm sorry. I only wanted for him to have a view," she said. "Look, just look what a beautiful view he has."

SINCE THAT DAY in 1972, I've attended two memorials for my father. The first was twenty-five years after Dad died, held by Local No. 4 in Golden Gate Park. They planted a sapling and dedicated the tree to my dad. Older men wept as they spoke of him as their leader and their friend. Younger men, who had never known him, came dressed in suits to show their respect for him. A Latina union official for Local No. 4 shook my hand. They'd been holding memorials for my father for years, I was surprised to hear.

"I didn't know," I said. "My mother didn't tell me."

The second was in 1996, held at Dad's tree in Golden Gate Park, to commemorate the thirtieth anniversary of his death. Willie Brown, an old political ally of Dad's, had just become Mayor of San Francisco and allowed the union to dedicate a bench in Dad's honor. The brass plaque on the bench was inscribed, "To others, he was a union leader. To us, he was a leader of men."

I spoke at the service, thanking the union. Afterward, two men who had been close to my father came to me. They clutched each other. One man wept unashamedly, tears streaming down his face.

"You *look* like your father," he said. "You move the way he did, and you have his voice."

AFTER I FOUND the box of clippings when I was nine years old, I no longer trusted my mother. She'd kept the facts of my father's death from me, and I'd *needed* her to tell me about him. Now I grilled her constantly, asking for details. I kept a list inside my head of the things about myself that people said were like my father's: hands, eyes, feet. Dad and I both liked to wear red, but our favorite color was blue.

On a Saturday night, Mom and I watched a showing of the film *Zorba the Greek* at the Bolinas Community Center. Afterward she said the character of Zorba was like my father. Then she went into her room and shut the door. Later that night, I snuck out of the house, and in the street I silently danced in the dark, doing Zorba's dance for my father.

He became my conscience. I imagined him watching me, like a spirit guide, or God. My father followed me; he stayed with me, became my second shadow.

When I was a few years older, twelve, my favorite baby-sitting job was taking care of a boy named Seth, who was eight. He was funny and smart and we read, talked, and wrestled like puppies. Seth's father was struck in a random shooting and died. Knowing about my dad, Seth's mother asked me to talk to him.

"Your father was murdered, too," she said. "Maybe you can talk to him about how you feel. Seth really loves you."

I felt like I'd been kicked in the chest—it was my mother who probably suggested it. But I didn't know how I felt about my dad being killed and had no idea what I was supposed to say. I tried to talk to Seth anyway. We were in his backyard. He had his back to me and was beating the fence with a stick. I reached out to touch him, but he moved away.

After that day, I could no longer stand to sit him. We saw ourselves, our loss, in each other's eyes; it hurt to be near.

7 · BACKWARD

SOMETIMES I LOVED my brother. Sometimes he was wild and full of life. Sometimes he brought me gifts and made promises to me I could believe. But he was unpredictable, turning dangerous in a flash. There was no warning, no time, before he exploded with violence. And when he did, I hated him with all my being. I grew wary of being alone with him, and when I was, I tried to get away fast. Things went better when I moved at the edge of his attention. But sometimes I was not fast enough.

I rode Shaheia most days after school. Lee was rarely home in the afternoon, but one day when I get home from school he's there. Some guy is sitting in the kitchen with him rolling a joint. I grab two apples and start back out the door.

"Where are you going?" Lee asks suddenly.

"Riding."

"When you gonna let me ride your horse?"

"You don't know how to ride. She won't let you get on her—she doesn't like men, remember?"

"That's bullshit." He mimics me, "*Hates men*—how do you know?"

"The girl who rode with us in Montana told me."

"We'll see about that," he said. "Besides, she's not even yours."

"She is so. Mom bought her for me."

"'She is so,'" he taunts. "You think *Mom* can afford a horse? I was the one who paid for that horse. I can take her away from you anytime I want to," he said. "Just like that." He snaps his fingers in my face.

"If you're gonna take her away, I'm gonna cut up your wet suit."

I drop the apples, grab my mother's kitchen scissors, and run upstairs to the bathroom, where Lee's wet suit is drying in the shower. I slam and lock the door, lower the toilet lid, sit down, and wait.

I hear Lee laughing downstairs. "Hold this doobie for me, man. I gotta teach my little sister a lesson."

I hear him come up the stairs. He pounds on the bathroom door.

"Open the door, Becky."

I don't move. He pounds harder.

"Open the fucking door."

Paralyzed, I clutch the scissors to my chest.

"Open—the—fucking—door." The wood splinters and begins to buckle toward me.

"OPEN—THE—FUCKING—DOOR—YOU—CUT—MY—WET SUIT—AND—YOU'RE—DEAD."

Lee kicks the door down. He punches me in the head, knocking me off the toilet seat. The scissors fly out of my hands and skitter across the floor.

"I didn't cut it," I say.

"Bitch," he says and kicks me in the stomach. "You fucking little bitch."

He kicks again, and I feel the breath leave my body. I try to get up.

"Don't you ever touch my stuff again. You owe me, you owe me for everything you have," Lee says.

Then he kicks me down the stairs. I go down head first, bouncing off the walls and the railings. I hit the bottom, scramble to my feet, and run.

I have to get to Shaheia before he does, to protect her. I know he can drive there much faster than I can run it. He could just go take her. I run through the fields, taking all the short cuts I know, sobbing out her name as I run. Coming down the hill, I see her across the field, grazing.

I call out, "Shaheia."

She raises her head and whinnies. I climb through the fence and stumble toward her. She shies and runs away from me. The other horses around her bolt, too. I run after them, crying, and I trip and fall. I see my mother's car coming down the road toward town and run across the pasture screaming and waving my arms, but she doesn't see me and doesn't stop.

I chase after her car and make it to the top of the Mesa. She is racing back toward me—I run out into the road. She brakes and jumps out.

"Jesus Christ," she says. "Get in the car."

"He said he was going to take Shaheia away," I sob. "He said he owned her."

"I know, I know what he said. I got home and that stoner was sitting there, puffing away. When he saw me, he said, 'Don't look at me, man, it was a fair fight.' I asked him, 'Who was fighting?' and he said, 'Your son and daughter'—how could he think that's a fair fight? You're a ten-year-old girl. Lee's a man, he's twenty-five years old."

I start to shake.

My mother wipes my face. "Shhh, now, I'll take care of it. When we get home, stay in the car until I call you."

We speed home. I crouch in the backseat and listen to my mother going down the walkway to the house. She calls, "Lee, get out here."

Lee runs out, shoves past my mother, gets in his Porsche, and speeds away.

I creep to my mother, and she hugs me.

"You must forgive him," she says. "You have to understand, Lee was supposed to go with your father the night he was killed, but your father and Lee got into a fistfight."

She tells me it had started the way their fights always began: at dinner. Lee said something provocative like "Pass the milk" instead of "Pass the milk, *please*," and my father took this as Lee being disrespectful. They fought, and Lee ran out of the house, and my father went to the meeting without him.

My mother pushes her glasses up and wipes her eyes. "Lee feels terrible guilt. He thinks that if he had gone, he could've stopped the killers—so you see, things have never been easy for Lee, not since that night."

My throat closes up. I want to yell, "What about me? Make him stop." But I know she won't. Lee will come back. She'll always let him come home.

After that beating, Lee got smarter. When Mom was not at home, he'd throw me against the wall, lean against it, and shake his finger or his fist in my face. "*Brat*," he'd rant. "*Stupid. Fat, fat, fat, spoiled, lazy, dumb.*"

He was relentless. While he ranted, I hummed and counted how many times he said "man."

"Man, you're so stupid." *One.*

"You think you have it tough? Man, when I was growing up in San Francisco with Dad . . ." *Two.*

"I'm the closest thing you have to a father, man—you better treat me with respect." *Three . . .*

I thought the counting protected me: If I counted, his words could not get to me. But I know now that they did get in. They lodged themselves in my spine, my heart.

Lee hit his girlfriends, too, women he brought home to live with us. Looking back, I cannot say which was worse— being hurt, or watching him hurt women I loved.

But for years I did not know how hurt I'd been and laughed when I told stories about my brother. I was puzzled by the sad looks on people's faces. I had pictures in my head of what had happened, but these had no feelings attached to them. The images ran in my imagination like short movies with no sound.

My fear of my brother would surface on even my best days with him. I was twenty-two and he was thirty-seven— I'd gone to Colorado to visit him and his wife and seven-year-old son. Lee drove me back to college in Southern California, and on the way we stopped at the Grand Canyon. We got a lucky break: There was one room at the inn at the bottom of the South Rim.

We smoked a joint and ran down the canyon at sunset, dodging hikers and mule trains. After dinner, when we were alone in our room, I sat on the edge of the bottom bunk bed to untie my boots, and suddenly I couldn't speak or move.

Lee reached out to touch me, and I recoiled. "What's the matter, Becky?" he asked sadly. "I'm not going to hurt you."

That night I lay awake in my bunk and listened to my brother breathe in the bunk above me.

After that trip, I knew I could never be alone with him again.

Five years later I was living with a beautiful man named Andrew in the lower story of his mother's house in Muir Beach, down the hill from the overlook where my father's ashes were buried. Andrew was well-educated, had two beautiful, fierce sisters and a mother who loved him. He was tall and had thick brown curly hair and a mustache. He was wonderful, except he sometimes drank too much.

On Friday and Saturday nights, while I waitressed in a seafood restaurant, Andrew hung out at his friend's house. He and his friends called it "The Pit." They drank, smoked dope, and listened to Jimi Hendrix and Van Morrison. Some nights Andrew didn't come home until three in the morning, while I lay in bed in rage.

One such night when he didn't come home, I drove down to The Pit. I was crying, and Andrew stumbled toward me to embrace me. He fell on me, and we both went over backward onto a coffee table. The table broke under us, and we hit the floor hard. Terrified, I pulled my leg up between us and kicked him across the room. His head cracked against the fireplace mantel, and he slid to the floor.

We both cried that night, both confused and frightened.

The next morning, I locked myself in the bathroom with the phone and called a battered women's hotline.

"I think I need help," I whispered to the counselor. "But I'm not sure you're the right people to call."

"Okay," the counselor said. "What kind of help do you think you need?"

"I think I might be a batterer," I said.

She asked me questions about the fight and my family.

"I think you have it backward," she said gently. "I think you were beaten."

My hands started to shake, and I almost dropped the phone.

"Really," I said, clutching the phone to my ear. "Are you sure?"

"Yes," she said. "I'm sure."

At the thirtieth-anniversary memorial for Dad, as the procession moved through Golden Gate Park, my brother sidled up to me.

"Have you forgiven me for the things I did to you?" Lee said.

"You haven't apologized yet," I said and walked faster.

A year later, he called to tell me he was a black belt in karate, and that part of his spiritual redemption was teaching self-defense classes for women.

"Can you imagine that?" he laughed. "Who better to teach it than me?"

Part of me thought it was perfect. The other part of me thought, *What a crock of shit.*

In another call he again asked if I'd forgive him.

"You won't even let me tell you how it felt," I said.

"Hey," he said, suddenly angry. "You have to let go of all that."

He repeated a parable his karate sensei had told him, then said, "For your own good, you have to forgive me."

"Sorry, you don't get to dictate this," I said and hung up.

But he kept trying. About once every six months to a year, he'd call. In one of these conversations I asked, "Why did you fight with Mom so much?" What I really meant, but was too afraid to ask, was, *Why do you hate women? Why did you hate me?*

"Let me tell you a secret," he said. "A few days after Dad was killed, I came home and Mom was having sex with this guy from the union—right there, on our living room floor. I freaked out. Dad had only been dead a few days, and no one knew who did it, or why. In that moment, I thought maybe *Mom* had Dad killed, so she could be with that man. Of course, she didn't—but she betrayed Dad, and she betrayed me."

I couldn't see this story. I didn't believe it. Maybe Lee was high; maybe Lee saw Mom being held by a man; maybe she even let him kiss her. I *could* see my mother, seeking comfort with that nameless man, trying to stay alive.

Lee and I worked our way up to a walk on the beach together. I was thirty-seven, Lee was fifty-two and the father of two children, yet I felt I needed to bring my two wolf-dogs with me for protection. My brother spoke of many things that day: his despair after Dad was killed, how differently his life turned out.

"What did you want to be?" I asked him.

"A poet," he said. "But, hey, I was an honorable smuggler. I never dealt dope to kids, I was good at it, and I got out before I got caught."

I frowned at his version, but didn't argue. Instead I asked, "Why do you want a relationship with me now?"

"You have this kind of emotional strength," he said. "I want my kids to know you."

I did not know what to say to this.

At some point, he forgot himself, got angry, and began to rant, and the wolves got between us with their ruffs up, barking. Lee backed away, his hands raised in submission.

"Did you love any of the women you beat up?" I said.

He looked at me sadly. "How could anyone call what I did 'love'?"

WHEN I WAS a child, the rock band Jefferson Starship bought the house at the west entrance to Bolinas Beach. They commissioned local artists to paint a mural along the concrete retaining wall beneath their house, facing the beach, where the surfers leaned their boards. Their house had one of the very few swimming pools in town, and sometimes they let us kids swim in it.

We'd pressed the buzzer on the black intercom box in front of their privacy gate. "Yes?" a disembodied female voice said, and we asked if we could swim in the pool. When she said yes, the electronic gate swung slowly open and we slid in. The pool was kidney-shaped and hand-tiled in tiny blue tiles. At the shallow end of the pool was a smiling orange and yellow sun, and at the deep end, a white crescent moon.

We dove down and kissed the sun on its lips and then swam and dove to the moon in deep water. We tried to catch a glimpse of the rock stars inside the house, but saw only shadowy forms, backlit by the sun-bright ocean behind them. After a while, a long-haired female groupie came out and told us it was time to go home.

The beach itself was divided: Half was a regular beach, and half a nude beach, where naked people lay on their towels in the sun or walked up and down the beach chatting.

At first, only locals went there. But then the nudie beach became famous. On the weekends, tourists came from over the hill. They stood on the bulkhead with binoculars, watching nude men play Frisbee and naked women running into the waves. A rumor went around town that our beach had been featured in a nudist magazine.

The locals grew angry, and a group of residents declared themselves the Bolinas Border Patrol. They wore T-shirts with a logo stenciled across the front, a black widow spider, and hung out in front of Smiley's Schooner Saloon on Friday and Saturday nights. They hassled tourists, let the air out of their tires, and took down the road signs to Bolinas.

When people asked us kids, "Is this Bolinas?" we'd say no and send them north to Point Reyes. "Just keep going, you're almost there."

And for all those years and to this day, the citizens would take down the road signs as soon as the highway people put them up. Amalia told me that she and one of her boyfriends were among the *very first* to do this—stoned, they rode out on a motorcycle, knocked the sign down, and dragged it into the ditch.

KARA, RUBY, AND I were fascinated by the topless surfer chicks on the nude beach who browned themselves with oils, Hawaiian coconut and Johnson's Baby Oil. We rode our horses past them and stared at their bare boobs when we thought they weren't looking. Kara stole a women's magazine from her older sister that featured a story about boobs. There was a double-sided foldout with photos of twenty topless women. Each woman's breasts were different: Some were high and tiny; some pointed upward; others were big and heavy-looking. Some nipples were pink, engorged; others, brown and hard as raisins. We each picked out the pair we wanted to have.

I did not want to have boobs like my mother's. I had seen her naked after her shower. Hers were large and covered with thin blue veins. Her round, white stomach puckered around the red line of her hysterectomy scar. I wanted small, high ones, also a flat, brown stomach, like the girls on the beach.

But we were still flat-chested and too embarrassed to sunbathe topless at the beach, so Ruby, Kara, and I lay out in Ruby's backyard or on my front deck.

"Girls," my mother called out, "you should put your tops on. Burned nipples hurt like hell."

"But Mom," I called back, "Tan lines are not cool."

"Well, then, be creative—stick Band-Aids on them, or flowers. That'll give you lovely little petal marks around your rosebuds. It can be your secret."

Giggling, Kara, Ruby, and I each picked two yellow daisies off of the bush in our front yard. We lay back down in the sun and carefully placed the flowers on our nipples. Every few minutes, we lifted our daisies up to check for our petals.

We three were riding on the beach one day when saw a naked man jacking off.

We reined around and charged him, yelling and waving our riding crops in the air.

The man jumped up, grabbed his clothes, and ran from the beach and into the street.

"Freak," we shouted. "Get out of our town."

Word spread through Bolinas: More perverts were coming to our beach. On the Mesa, one woman was raped, then another. The county sheriff called a town meeting at the community center.

"Why do I have to go?" I asked my mother.

"Because I want you to hear what the sheriff has to say," she said. "I don't want you to be afraid, but I want you to be safe."

Bolinas was too small to have its own police station; we only had a sheriff's deputy who cruised around town and up and down the Mesa. When he drove past and waved at Kara, Ruby, and me, we reluctantly waved back at him, and when he was past us, we looked at each other and said, "Whew, that was close."

The community center was crowded and hot. People were tense and angry and calling out questions.

"Please, calm down," the sheriff said. "We're doing everything we can."

"Aww, bullshit," a man called out. "If you can't take care of it, the Border Patrol will." People started shouting and pointing at the sheriff and his deputy.

My mother stood up. "Okay, time to go," she said and pushed me toward the door.

"What's going to happen, Mom?" I asked.

"Nothing, don't worry, nothing's going to happen."

Later that night, Lee cornered me and said, "Stay away from the beach this weekend."

"Why?"

"Just stay away," he said.

Later, the whole town heard what happened. On Saturday, a group of men appeared at the top of the cliff overlooking the crowded nudie beach. They wore hats, sunglasses, and bandannas tied over the bottoms of their faces. From the cliff, they pelted the nudies with eggs.

My mother asked Lee. "Were you involved in this vigilante thing?"

Lee laughed and raised his hands. "No way, Mom. Honest."

Then he winked at me, smiled.

8 · THE JOY OF SEX

WHEN I WAS eleven, Amalia got pregnant for the second time. Mom was very upset.

"I don't care if you have sex," she said to me. "But don't get pregnant."

"Mom, I'm only *eleven*," I said, mortified.

I already knew some things about sex. In the summer, the Goreks came up from Echo Park to visit us for a week. While the adults were downstairs drinking wine and smoking pot, we locked ourselves in my bedroom and played The Nudie Club. We took off our clothes and jumped on the bed. The summer I was eight, The Nudie Club ended when Roy, the eldest Gorek boy, turned thirteen. He didn't want to take of his clothes.

"My body has changed," he said. "You'll laugh at me."

"No," we all swore. "We won't."

"Well, okay," he said.

He slowly unzipped his pants and pulled them down. His dick was long, his crotch covered with curly black hair.

We squealed, and Roy quickly pulled his pants back on. "I *told* you! you promised you wouldn't laugh."

We ran in circles around him, chanting, "Roy has a big dick, Roy has a big dick."

For a while, we had a second dog, Blossom, and before Mom could have her spayed, she went into heat and all the male dogs in Bolinas showed up at our house. My mother chased them off and locked Blossom on the back deck. She nailed a six-foot wire barricade across the steps to keep the dogs out. Eventually, all the dogs gave up except one black lab. He scaled the fence, but I caught him just as he reached the top. My mother whacked him with a broom, and he fell back.

But he wouldn't give up, and the next time I checked, he and Blossom had their back ends stuck together. Mom got out the hose and sprayed them. The lab ran in circles, dragging Blossom along like a pushmi-pullyu, while I whacked him with the broom.

Blossom got pregnant, and when she went into labor, my mom loaded us into the Bug, driving fourteen miles north to the vet in Point Reyes, but Blossom gave birth to the first puppy in the car, on my lap, delivering the puppy into my hands. "Good job," the vet later told me, as she helped Blossom deliver her second pup.

I also knew about sex from Sammie, one of the most popular girls in town. Kara, Ruby, and I didn't much like playing with her because she was bossy and made us take what she called "manhood tests." Like climb up the cliff from Agate Beach, stand in the tide pools while the tide came in, crawl through poison oak and mud, or go into the cave she found up the hill behind the Bolinas Store, at dusk without a flashlight.

Sammie invited us to sleep over at her house and see the ghost of Isadora Duncan. She told us that Isadora Duncan died right in front of the place when her long white scarf got caught in the wheel of her sports car and "strangled her totally to death." She swore that the ghost danced in her house every night.

"It happens after midnight—the music starts, and you can hear her footsteps. Shhhh," she whispered. "Do you hear it?"

"I don't hear anything," Ruby said. "You're making this up."

"Now you've done it," Sammie said. "You scared the ghost away. She's gone."

Then she pulled a book out from under her bed. "Look what I have," she said. It was *The Joy of Sex*. "It's my mother's. It's got pictures of people doing it."

We looked at the pictures by flashlight. The drawings detailed genitalia, sexual postures—we were both disgusted and mesmerized.

Amalia and Luis were living near Santa Rosa, and Luis kept a stack of *Playboy*s hidden in the bathroom closet at their house. On our rare visits to their house, I snuck in there and looked at them. The women in them were smooth and pink. They lay on couches and over chairs, in filmy outfits, spreading their legs wide and cupping their boobs. Mostly I stared at their boobs. I was secretly worried about my boobs, worried I wasn't going to get them, or that they would be huge or misshapen.

I had a crush on a boy then, Joe McBride. He was tall and quiet and always wore a red or blue bandanna neatly tied around his forehead. I'd had a crush on him since the third grade, when he gave me a string of love beads for my birthday. Once, at a party at his parents' house, we snuck off with a half bottle of cheap burgundy and made ourselves sick. But we had never kissed.

Joe and I and other Bolinas kids went to camp that summer. Forest Farm Camp was in Forest Knolls, northeast of Bolinas, less than an hour's drive, but for us, this was a world away. We were isolated in Bolinas, even from the kids in Stinson, but at camp there would be kids from other towns to play with. We were all terribly excited. But just days before camp there was an outbreak of hepatitis C in Bolinas. The other schools canceled, believing the Bolinas kids were contagious.

At camp, we were not allowed to swim. The gate to the pool was closed and padlocked. On the hottest days we hung on the chain-link fence and stared at the perfect, blue water.

The counselors divided us into cabins: two cabins for the boys and two for the girls. The girls' cabins immediately made war on each other. Desperate to keep us occupied, the counselors taught us to square dance. The girls loved the calls and the near gallop of the dances. We loved to do-si-do.

When we got to Ladies' Choice time, the boys stood in a circle with their eyes closed and the counselor called out, "Ladies, go and stand behind the boy you most want to dance with."

I rushed over and stood behind Joe. I couldn't wait for him to turn around and see me; I hopped from foot to foot.

"Now, gentlemen," the counselor called out, "Turn around, and open your eyes."

Joe opened his eyes, looked at me, and fainted.

The counselor rushed over. He slapped Joe to bring him round, and pulled him to his feet. "Stop fooling around. This girl wants to dance with you."

Joe fainted again. Two counselors half-carried him off of the dance floor. I stood frozen, until a counselor said, "Okay, everybody, stop staring," and then I bolted, like a deer.

Years later, Joe and I bumped into each other at a party. "What happened that day?" I asked.

He blushed. "I turned around and saw you, and you were beaming," he said. "And, well, it was—you were—just *too much*."

IN RESPONSE TO Amalia's pregnancy, my mom organized a birth control class for the girls in Bolinas. Our living room was packed with girls, ages eleven to seventeen. I was eleven, and Ruby and Kara were twelve; we three were the youngest in the room and sat together on the carpet, giggling and nudging each other. The older girls flushed, trying to look superior. My mom introduced her friend Judy, who worked for Planned Parenthood.

"Sex is something that you'll enjoy," my mom told the assembled girls. "The important thing is to not get pregnant. That's why we're here today."

Judy passed around pictures of male and female anatomy and talked about sex. She did not use my mother's words, *bosoms*, *crotch*, *bottom*, or—my favorite—*tuchas*, or words Ruby, Kara, and I sometimes used, *dick*, *butt*, *screw*, or words we heard adults say, *pussy*, *fuck*, *head*, *come*. Judy used Latin and Greek words, *labia*, *penis*, and formal words, *oral sex*, *penetration*, *ejaculation*, *orgasm*. She called having sex *making love*. Then she handed out condoms, diaphragms, IUDs, and packets of pills.

"Don't expect a man to be responsible for birth control," she said. "Everyone can get carried away in the moment. You have to take care of yourselves. I want you to handle these things, so you get used to the idea of using them."

She demonstrated by uncapping a tube of spermicidal jelly and sniffing it. "See: It doesn't smell bad." A tiny blob of jelly stuck to the end of her nose, but she ignored it. A low giggle ran through the room.

"Let's talk about masturbation," Judy said.

We fell silent.

"Any questions?"

Women who were in that class still talk about how great it was—educational, candid, and liberating. When Kara, Ruby, and I talk about it, we roll our eyes and revert back to the eleven- and twelve-year-old girls that we were.

Mom dated a few times, but she never had a serious relationship with a man after my father died. Only once did she mention a man to me.

"There's a man from your dad's union—he's offered to marry me, help raise you," she said. She did not say his name.

"He has a swimming pool, you could have a swimming pool," she said to me. "Would you like that?"

"No," I said.

"Fine," she said. "I thought I'd let you choose."

Once, she told Amalia she had decided to become a lesbian.

"Okay," Amalia said, trying not to laugh. "But I don't think it works that way."

After Amalia got married and had children, I rarely got to see her, even though she and Luis lived only an hour away, near Santa Rosa. Mom kept us apart. When I asked to see my sister, Mom said, "She has her hands full." In turn, she told Amalia I was angry with her and didn't want to see her.

As mad as Mom was at Amalia for having babies, she loved being a grandmother. Amalia's oldest son, Jason, adored his grandma Barbara. His favorite story about her is when he came to visit us with his friend Todd. Jason and Todd were riding their bikes across the Mesa, and Todd rode right off the cliff. Jason raced back to the house and got my mother. They drove back in Mom's Volkswagen Bug. She threw a rope down to Todd and tied the other end to her back fender.

"Tie the rope to the front of your bike," she told Todd. "Now get on, and hang on tight to the handlebars," and she towed him up the cliff.

"I love my grandma Barbara," Jason said. "She's the best grandma in the world."

WHEN MY MOTHER got her teaching credential, she took a yearlong position at a state-run school in Ukiah for developmentally disabled kids; this was 125 miles north of Bolinas. She, Shaheia, Puppers, and I moved into a dusty white trailer in the midst of fifty-five acres outside Redwood Valley, a small town just north of Ukiah. The trailer was down a long dirt road and through two gated fences. The fenced acreage served as a pasture for Shaheia, and I had lots of room to ride.

Our landlady drove a battered pickup truck with a shotgun rack in the rear window. She warned us about rattlesnakes and said they liked to nest sometimes under our trailer. "Watch for them when you ride," she said. "Your horse will sense them before you do." Once, when Mom and I were eating dinner, the landlady showed up and searched for rattlesnakes under our trailer, a flashlight in one hand and the shotgun over her shoulder. My mother and I watched her from the porch. She finally gave up and drove away. "What an odd woman," Mom said. "I think she might have a drinking problem."

I went to school in Redwood Valley, a very different place from Bolinas School. In Bolinas, we learned how to build, sew, plant, draw, make jewelry, write, and sing. Oh, how we sang—traditional folk and slave songs, gospel hymns, the best of James Taylor. In Redwood Valley, you needed a pass to go to the bathroom. The principal had two spanking paddles hung on the wall behind his desk.

My fifth-grade teacher was named Mr. Wall. He had blurred, bluish Navy tattoos on his arms. We sat at desks in straight rows, and when we practiced our handwriting, Mr. Wall walked around the room with a ruler. If you held your pencil too close to the lead, he whacked your hand, sending the pencil flying across the room. Then he would say, "Go pick it up and try again."

There was an older kid named Danny in our class. The other kids told me he had been held back in fifth grade four times and that Mr. Wall picked on him.

"Danny here is not so smart, are you, Danny?" Mr. Wall said.

Danny would hang his head and stare at his desk. "No, sir," he would mumble. "I'm not smart."

"That's right—and you're going to stay right here in this classroom until you get smart."

The third week of school, during Geography, Mr. Wall asked Danny to name the capital of California.

"I don't remember, sir," Danny said.

"You don't remember? How many times have you taken this class?" Mr. Wall said. He reached down and grabbed Danny by the back of his pants and his collar and lifted him out of his seat. He carried Danny up to the blackboard and held his face in front of the question chalked on the board.

"What is the capital of California?" Mr. Wall slammed Danny's head into the blackboard.

The class froze.

He slammed Danny into the blackboard again. "Answer the question."

"I don't know, Mr. Wall," Danny sobbed.

I told Mom what happened, and she moved me to another school. She said the teaching practices there were barbaric. At the new school, I was asked out on my first date. A boy named Ron asked me to a movie. Later, I heard kids talking about going to the movies just to make out, and about the boys "feeling up" the girls. I was anxious about being felt up, so I met Ron at the movie theater dressed in a shirt buttoned to my neck, a sweater, a double-breasted Navy pea coat, and a knit cap.

"Why are you wearing so many clothes?" he asked. "Aren't you hot?"

MOM OFTEN BROUGHT me with her to work in the afternoons after school and sometimes on weekends. "You can help," she said. "You can be their role model."

Her class was a catch-all for all kinds of kids with mental disabilities, and—at first—I was frightened. I was startled by the way they moved, some rocking back and forth, some drooling, and their loud, shrill voices. But I learned how to talk to them, and we played blocks and colored with crayons—things little kids did.

She focused her work on severely autistic kids, especially infants, and started building learning environments for them. Some of the infants she worked with could not hold their heads up, and so to help them, recalling the Tactile Dome in the Exploratorium, she filled tubs with birdseed and buried the babies up to their necks. Her idea was that the birdseed would support their bodies so they could look up and out, but the birdseed made too much dust and the babies sneezed. She tried rice, but that made them sneeze, too. Then she tried lentils, which worked. The babies looked like bodyless little heads, craning their necks and peering out at the world.

There was one baby in particular, a boy named Johnny—my mother loved Johnny. He had terrible seizures, and Mom was trying to find out what caused them and how to help him. His parents were young and very poor and completely overwhelmed. She gave Johnny's parents our phone number. When Johnny had a seizure, they called my mother, and she went to help them.

At the institution, I discovered a floor of kids waiting to be placed in foster homes. I was given special permission to play with them during certain hours and on Saturdays. My mom said they'd been taken from their families for different reasons, that they were now wards of the state. They were not allowed to go outside unsupervised because they were considered flight risks—many of them had already run away from home, or other institutions—so we played cards, jacks, jump rope. The boys and girls slept in separate, locked dormitories.

I asked Betsy, the best jacks player, "What did you guys do?"

"Me? I'm here for shoplifting. See him? He stole a car, and her," she pointed to a girl jumping rope, "She's in for prostitution. Does that *bother* you?"

"No," I said, passing her the ball. "Here, it's your throw."

The girls I went to school with were all part of Girl Scouts, and I desperately wanted to join, too. My mother was not in favor of this, saying Girl Scouts was about learning to be a "Goody Two-shoes." Instead, she wanted me to join Camp Fire Girls. She'd been a leader of a Camp Fire troop, teaching girls camping and outdoor survival skills. Also, she and Dad had taken groups of inner-city kids camping.

Both my parents had loved to camp, and my father had also loved to hunt. Mom had lots of black-and-white snapshots of Dad in his padded hunting vest, his arms around Lee and Amalia, with dead ducks slung around their necks. There were a couple of photos of me, too, a fat baby in a playpen under some trees. But there were no photos of me and my father.

There were no Camp Fire troops in Ukiah, so my mother reluctantly allowed me to join the Girl Scouts, and to her relief, I didn't last long. Our troop did not go camping and mostly worked on badges for cooking and sewing. They let me be the flag bearer, and when I fooled around and let the American flag touch the ground, they kicked me out. Mom tried not to act too pleased, but I knew she was.

WHEN MOM'S CONTRACT was up, we went home to Bolinas and Mom got a state grant to work with an orphaned girl named Penny, a physically disabled, autistic fifteen-year-old.

Penny had dark brown hair, cut in a rough pageboy. She wore glasses with black frames and thick, Coke-bottle lenses. Penny dragged her right foot on the ground when she walked and kept her right wrist pulled up to her chin, fingers splayed. Her head was always tilted to one side, and sometimes she drooled onto the back of her hand. Penny loved music and would listen to it carefully. If it excited her, she'd grunt or squeal or laugh. She communicated by nodding *yes*, or shaking her head *no*.

Mom resolved to teach Penny to speak, confident that with her light and sound environments and music lessons, she could coax Penny to at least sing.

"Penny chooses not to interact with the world," she told me. "I'm going to teach her that it's okay to be in the world, and to speak."

My mother arranged for the two of us to have piano lessons together in Oakland, near where Penny lived. Again, Mom said I was to be the role model. Gretchen, the piano teacher, was studying to be a music therapist.

I was not very good at piano. I bashed my way through "The Alley Cat Song" or "The Pink Panther Theme," as Penny cocked her head and listened.

"Did you practice, Becky?" Gretchen asked, exasperated.

"Yes," I said.

"Well, clearly not enough."

Penny didn't have to practice. She'd listen to me play a piece once and sit down at the piano and play it perfectly. No sheet music, no help from the teacher.

Mother said, "You're such a talented girl!" as she smiled and stroked the back of Penny's head. I was terribly jealous of Penny, of her talent, and the gentle way my mother loved her.

After our lesson, we'd sit at Gretchen's kitchen table and try to make Penny talk. My mother peeled a banana and an orange, and Penny got excited and began to rock back and forth. Mom held out a piece of banana.

"Say *please*, Penny. I know you can, I know you know the word."

Penny bobbed her head and squealed in frustration.

Mother turned to me. "Becky, say *please*."

I crossed my arms. "Please," I said flatly.

"Don't be a snot," Mom said. "You have to demonstrate how to do it."

"Okay, may I please have a piece of banana?"

Penny squealed again and reached for the banana on the table.

"Maybe she doesn't want to talk," I said. "Maybe you shouldn't make her."

My mother glared at me. "Of course she wants to talk. If you can't help, then just be quiet."

Mom regularly filmed her work with Penny. One afternoon, she set the camera on a tripod and said we were all going to dance. Later, after she viewed the footage, she decided to show it to Penny.

"She needs to see herself," Mom said. "She's so internal and self-referential, I don't think she has a sense of herself as a whole person, in relation to other people. We can watch it together."

She and Gretchen tacked a white sheet on Gretchen's living room wall. In the film, Penny, my mother, Gretchen, and I held hands as we danced in a circle. Mom raised Penny's hand up in the air as she led her, step-by-step. Penny shuffled along beside Mother and laughed.

"Look," she whispered to Penny, pointing at the screen. "Look, look up there. Who's that?"

Penny squealed and buried her head in my mother's lap. She looked up shyly at the screen.

"Who's that, Penny? Who is that beautiful, dancing girl?"

I stared up at the images and ground my teeth in jealousy.

Penny lived in a rundown house with Mrs. Owens, her foster mother, and six other handicapped children, all of them wards of the state. Mrs. Owens received state funds for each child she took in. My mother said she was making a mint of money.

My mother thought that Penny would not talk because Mrs. Owens was neglecting or abusing her, and she plotted to catch the woman at it. She made sneak visits to her house, showing up early or even unannounced to pick Penny up.

"When Mrs. Owens opens the door," my mother said, "get in the house as fast as you can, and get a good look around."

"For what?"

"Just do it," she said and hit the door buzzer.

The house smelled like grilled cheese sandwiches and Campbell's vegetable soup. The children were seated at a yellow Formica table eating lunch. A small girl, wearing a bib, was flinging food on the floor. The other children, including Penny, ignored her. Mom called Penny to her, and Mrs. Owens and Mom both smiled, teeth bared. Mom sent me out into the backyard with a new boy named Andy while she and Mrs. Owens talked.

Andy looked normal to me. "How old are you?" I said.

"Ten," he said. "Ten, I'm ten." He picked up an old piece of clothesline and twisted it into a noose.

"I'm twelve," I said, watching his hands. "What do you want to play?"

"The devil is inside me, and I have to kill him," Andy said. He put the rope around his own neck and pulled it tight.

I leapt onto him, knocked him down, and called for my mom. Andy cried and curled up in a ball. My mom and Mrs. Owens lifted him and carried him inside.

After they sedated him, Mom tried to explain to me what happened. "Andy has hallucinations," she said. "I know this was scary, but right now you have to try to act normal for Penny—she's at a crucial stage in her development of trust—do you understand?"

I hung my head and kicked the ground. "Yes," I said.

But I was angry and blamed Penny, and when we were all in the car, when my mother wasn't looking, I reached over and pinched Penny's arm very hard.

9 · TROUBLE AND LIES

I ONCE TOLD LEE a memory I had of Dad, where he swung me up onto his shoulders. We sang all the way to the corner store, and he bought me candy, a rainbow of Pixy Stix.

Lee looked stunned. "That wasn't Dad," he said. "That was me."

I was shocked—could I have misremembered? Maybe Lee did carry me, but surely my father must have carried me, too. We must have sung together, my dad and I.

When I think of my brother, I don't think of siblings playing. We were too far apart in age for much of that. Instead, I think of his intense physicality, his consuming vibe. There is a scene in the movie *Blow* where cocaine-smuggling George Jung, played by Johnny Depp, goes through customs at the airport. Depp is dressed in white and wearing sunglasses, all swagger and cool. As an adult, watching Depp, I thought, *That's my brother*.

I HAVE A picture of me and Lee, taken at my thirteenth birthday party, which was a costume party. I'm a flat-chested Catwoman, dressed in a black leotard, stockings, high heels with little rhinestone buckles, and long black plastic fingernails. Ruby is a busty Wonder Woman, with silver stars spray-painted across her chest. We stand on either side of Lee, with our hips cocked. He is dressed as a pimp, in a thigh-length fur coat and a maroon Super Fly hat with a long plume. His legs are bare, and he's wearing Dr. Scholl's wooden sandals.

LEE GAVE ME a grocery bag full of pot leaves.

"It's better that you learn about dope from me—but don't tell Mom."

When I called Kara to tell her, she said, "That's just like your brother to give you leaf and keep the buds—what a cheapskate. I'll be right over."

We heard that baking pot made it stronger, so we made dope chocolate cookies. We crumbled in so many leaves, the cookies turned green. "Do you feel anything?" I asked after we each ate one. "Not really," Kara said. We were too afraid to eat more.

I put the plate of cookies up on a shelf, and we went Downtown. In the morning, the plate was almost empty. Mom had eaten them in the middle of the night.

She had a terrible sweet tooth. When she was not home, I often crawled into her bed and hunted for the half a Hershey's chocolate bar or box of black licorice stashed under her pillows. At the movies, she loved to eat Jordan almond candies and Bit-O-Honey bars. She always had a pack of Juicy Fruit or Doublemint gum, which she chewed half a stick at a time.

I knocked on her bedroom door. "Mom, are you okay?"

"Wow," she said. "Get me a bucket."

She spent two days in bed. I was sure she'd kick me out, but when she recovered she said, "The next time you put dope in your cookies, write me a note."

LEE LIVED WITH his girlfriend Gloria in a cabin he built in our front yard. We christened it "The Fort." On the day they moved in, my mother and I watched from our deck.

"Now I'll never get rid of him," she sighed.

Gloria had long, sandy-blond hair and bangs—she was tiny, full of energy.

"She's feisty, that one," my mother said approvingly.

Gloria let me dress up in her clothes, even though I was growing rapidly and was already taller than she. Her beautiful, flowered dresses were too tight for me, and my feet were snug in her shoes.

Gloria always hugged me and said, "Oh, you look so beautiful."

Gloria and Lee played tennis in Downtown Bolinas. Lee, a natural athlete who loved surfing, skiing, and tennis, was teaching Gloria to play. I heard stories about their fights on the court. When people talked about my brother, they looked over their shoulders first. In one fight, she spat at him and he leapt over the net and hit her in the face with his racket. She had cuts on her face and a black eye. When I saw her, I cried.

She tried to smile. "Your brother just has a bad temper," she said, hugging me. "I guess I shouldn't have spit at him."

"*Goddamn* him," my mother said.

I once found Gloria doubled up on the floor of The Fort. "Are you okay?" I cried, kneeling beside her.

"He kicked me in the belly. I might be hemorrhaging."

"I'm gonna call Mom."

She grabbed my arm. "No, just help me get in bed. We'll call her if it gets worse—really, I'll be fine."

Gloria was okay that day, but their fights continued.

WE HAD A new school bus driver that year, a Vietnam veteran. Al was a short man with a muscular body and hair that fell to his waist. When we kids fought on the bus, he'd rage, shouting, "Goddammit. Shut up," and swerve the bus over to park on the side of the road, then throw the door lever, opening the doors with a hydraulic hiss, and storm off the bus into a nearby field. We'd all watch as Al strode up and down, clenching and unclenching his hands, shaking his fists at the sky, long hair swinging like a girl's. Shocked into stillness, we waited quietly in our seats until he calmed down, got back on, and started the engine. We rode the rest of the way home in silence.

We were curious about the war and about him, so a group of us twelve- and thirteen-year-olds once knocked on Al's door. He invited us in and we sat on his living room floor and smoked a bong. He told us a story about Vietnam.

He'd driven tanks. He and a friend were ordered by their commanding officer to steer their tanks through a field they knew was riddled with land mines. It was suicide, and they refused. The officer threatened them with arrest if they disobeyed the direct order. Al still refused, but his friend complied. The friend hit a mine, his tank blew up.

"He was in pieces," Al said, shaking his head. Al attacked the officer, beat him badly. "Sometimes I wish I'd killed him."

We sat, rapt, not knowing what to say. One of the boys passed Al the bong again, and he took a long hit.

No one in our families had been in the war, but my brother had received a draft notice to report. Lee said he and Mom came up with a plan to evade it. Before his interview, he dropped acid and smeared chunky peanut butter on his ass crack. In his interview, he leapt up on the table and dropped his pants, and they threw him out.

FOR THREE YEARS running, the Bolinas-Stinson School scored the lowest in the state on standardized exams. The downside to our alternative education was showing itself—we were hugely creative, but we did not test well. The California Board of Education was adamant that we bring up our test scores. The first group targeted to improve was mine, the sixth-through-eighth-grade combination.

In addition to not performing well academically, our class was factionalized, fighting with each other, inside and outside of school. Boys fought with boys and girls with girls, but "chick fights" were the worst. The cool, hard surfer chicks often started them. They already had budding breasts and wore tight jeans and T-shirts without bras. They tossed their hair when they walked and smoked pot with the boys down by the creek behind school.

Chick fights were scary to be in and almost as scary to watch. The girls fought dirty: They hissed and clawed and tore at each other's clothes—but I didn't fight with girls. I fought with boys.

We played volleyball during lunch, with our teachers, and we taunted each other. After one game, I walked up to a boy we called Spanky, the best spiker, and said, "Fat boy."

He grabbed me by the hair and lifted me off the ground. Kids chanted, "Fight! Fight!"

I hung there, spitting and trying to kick him.

"Not so tough now, are you?" he said.

The bell rang, and everyone scattered. The principal ran toward us across the playground, shouting. Spanky dropped me. I fell onto my knees and lunged at him.

"She started it," Spanky said.

The principal hauled us off to his office. "Jesus," he said. "You kids have got to stop fighting."

I fought with my math teacher, Mr. Stillman, too. When he asked me to sit in a chair, I sat on the table, smiled, and swung my legs back and forth.

"Get off the table," Mr. Stillman said. "Now."

"No," I said, "you can't make me."

Mr. Stillman pulled me off the table. The class fell silent, watching us struggle, until Mr. Stillman marched me out of class.

After a conference with my mother, a teacher's assistant named Linda was assigned to help me. Linda was soft-spoken, with large brown eyes. Twice a week, she'd take me out of class and we'd go sit in the garden and talk about my anger.

She gave me a small blue notebook in which to keep a journal. "I want you to write down what you feel," she said. "When you feel angry, excuse yourself from class. I want you to write about your anger, write until you feel better. You don't need to show your journal to anyone, it's yours."

The first time I left class with my journal, I was embarrassed. I thought everyone was watching me. I sat on the empty baseball field and opened the notebook, but I didn't know how to start. Finally, I wrote *I hate you I hate you I hate you*. I wrote the words larger and larger, until there was only one word on each page: *I. HATE. YOU.*

I got up and started to spin, arms outstretched. I imagined the kids in the classroom watching me through the smoked windows—this was the kind of glass you can see out of, but not into. I spun until the buildings and the trees blurred. I spun faster, made myself bigger, faster, stronger. I was bigger than Lee. I imagined pinning him against the wall, like he pinned me, raising my fist to his head and laughing, "How do you like it?" I punched out at the air. "How stupid do you feel now?"

Sometimes I fantasized about going to San Quentin. I fly there; I have wings. I find Rasnick, the mastermind. I grasp the bars that separate us and say, "Do you know who I am? I am Dow Wilson's youngest child." He cowers before me as I raise my sword and burst into flames.

In our homeroom, we played a survival game: "Imagine you're flying in an airplane," said Mrs. Tolle, our teacher. "It crashes into a mountain and some of you are hurt. Somebody must go for help. Choose four people, two boys and two girls, to lead you through this crisis." I was chosen as one of the four.

"Now, follow Mr. Stillman, please," Mrs. Tolle said.

We strutted proudly behind Mr. Stillman as he led us to the library. A man and woman were waiting for us, and Mr. Stillman quickly left the room. We eyed the strangers.

"Please, sit down." The man gestured to four chairs across from him and the woman. "My name is Mark, and this is my associate Jean."

Warily, we sat down.

"We were hoping to talk with you today about feelings. I know that, as a man, I sometimes have trouble expressing my feelings." He crossed his legs and pulled at his sock.

"We're psychiatrists," Jean said, glancing at Mark. "And your principal sent for us. We understand that you four are very independent." They asked us about our feelings about our fathers and authority.

We glanced at each other—realizing we'd been tricked. The doctors wanted to see the *troublemakers*, not the leaders. We got up and walked out, we were acting tough, but I was scared.

Maybe something *was* wrong with me. Sometimes I got so angry I couldn't see, my vision narrowed and darkened, my ears roared, and I struck out with my fists in fear, desperation.

My mother wanted me to drop out of school. She talked about buying a small Chinook RV and traveling across the country, just the two of us.

My choices? Neither was good: I didn't want to be in trouble at school anymore or go on the road with my mom.

And then we got a new English teacher, whose name was Ellen—we called all our teachers by their first names.

Ellen was thin, stoop-shouldered. She wore glasses and had a low, rich smokers' laugh. She had crooked teeth.

The first time I saw Ellen, I was sitting by myself at the far end of the basketball court, writing in my journal. As I watched her walk toward me across the schoolyard I thought, *This person may change my life.*

Ellen was loud—she laughed a lot. She was smart and quick, but not easily angered. When she did lose her temper, she turned red in the face and shook. She loved to play volleyball; she had a mean serve and a great spike. She was passionate, firm, and fair. I wanted desperately to please her.

For my first English report I wrote about the dancer Fred Astaire. I carefully copied a sequence of Fred Astaire dancing onto the cover of my report. The only detail I remember is that Astaire weighed 140 pounds. I got a B+. For Ellen, I worked hard. School, with Ellen in it, was better.

I CONTINUED TO question my mom about my father. "Didn't he know what he was doing was dangerous?" I said, meaning but not saying, *Why didn't you see his murder coming?*

"President Kennedy had been assassinated in 1963, and we were still in shock—the whole country was in shock," she said. "We never dreamed it would happen to us."

Mom tried to help me in her own way. She tried to give me information about things that scared me. She took me to meet prominent San Francisco attorney Terence Hallinan. When we were seated in his office, Terence said, "Becky, when you are ready, you can come see me, and I'll tell you about your father's murder."

Which only made me more confused: What did *ready* mean? How would I know when I was *ready*?

She also planned to take me to a heart specialist. I was born with a heart murmur—I'd been told. When I was born the doctor told my parents that if I didn't have open-heart surgery *right then*, I might die. On the other hand, there was a strong chance that I wouldn't survive the surgery.

"I thought I was going to lose you, too," my mother said. "And I could not bear to lose another baby, but your father didn't give up."

The weekend before we went to see the heart specialist, Amalia came to visit. When Mom was out of the room, I repeated to Amalia what she had told me.

Amalia gave a sharp bark of laughter.

"Did she tell you that she committed herself to a psychiatric ward? They gave her shock treatments, drugs. She left me and Dad and Lee to take care of you—don't get me wrong, I loved taking care of you. You were like a giant doll I got to play with, I bathed and dressed you.

"Dad took you to doctor after doctor, until he found one who said you would be fine. There's nothing wrong with you."

She was right. My heart was fine—but I'm still haunted by those images, my mother, electrified, and my father, carrying me from doctor to doctor, like an offering.

10 · A GOOD ENEMY

MY MOTHER LOVED hardware stores. She loved flea markets and RadioShack, and she loved to sing. She loved Vivaldi, Bob Marley, and Led Zeppelin. At Christmastime, she liked to go to a big discount store like Cost Plus and key up the windup toys and send them down the aisles.

She was famous for her tolerance for crazy people, for being flamboyant and loyal. Her friend Annie said, "If I told your mother about someone being mean to me, she'd actively hate them on my behalf, and I loved her for that."

Of politics Mom said, "Never forget that the far right and the far left are exactly the same." When General Franco died, she cried.

"Why are you crying?" I asked. "You should be happy."

"You always cry when a good enemy dies," she said. "A good enemy is the one you can see—it's the ones you can't see who are the most dangerous."

She also told me not to worry about getting boobs. "Don't be in such a rush," she said.

Ruby got hers first. She started dressing in halter tops and tube tops, sunbathing on her back porch in a tiny white bikini. Her older brother's friends gathered at their house every afternoon to smoke pot and watch sports, while Ruby, in her bikini, ignored their hungry stares as she paraded by.

Kara and Ruby were a year ahead of me in school, so now they were going over the hill to Tamalpais High in Mill Valley. Before my freshman year, when I would then join them, Ruby gave me a tour of the school. It was lunchtime and students were lying all over the grass, talking and laughing.

"That's the gym," Ruby said. "That's the front steps, where all the jocks and cheerleaders hang out. Most everybody from Bolinas and Stinson hangs out by the shop buildings or in the back parking lot—I don't, but everyone calls us 'Bobo Burnouts,' no matter where we hang out."

Ruby was wearing a scarlet tube top, skintight jeans, and platform shoes. As we walked, two tall guys appeared on either side of Ruby. They lifted her up by either elbow and started singing "Well she's a brick house, she's mighty mighty / Just lettin' it all hang out."

"Help," Ruby said. "Put me down."

They set her down and backed away, snapping their fingers and singing, "Shake it down, down / Shake it."

"Assholes," Ruby said, but she was smiling.

I'd prayed to get breasts like Ruby's. In eighth grade, the boys called me a carpenter's dream—flat as a board. But then I started to develop. My new boobs were perfect, small, just what I wanted, but I kept developing, until I was a 36 DD cup. Ruby's older brother, Rob, stared at my new chest and said, "Wow, *you* sure have changed."

In fact, my whole body swelled and exploded. Clothes no longer fit, everything suddenly now too short, too tight. In the dressing room at Macy's department store, my mother watched me struggle into a larger brassiere.

"Well, you finally got your bosoms," she said. "What you don't know is, your whole life's just changed."

BEFORE I STARTED Tam High, the older kids warned me not to say I was from Bolinas. Some teachers were rumored to be biased against us; they thought we were poor, rowdy, ignorant. Ellen, our Bolinas School teacher, went to meet with teachers at Tam High, asking them not to prejudge us. My first day, I saw group of Bolinas boys hanging out near a walkway. As the other kids surged by, those boys stood there, looking very lost and very stoned. They raised their chins in vague greeting as I passed.

I did not lie, but I watched my teachers for signs of prejudice. There was another group of kids who did not easily fit. They were from Marin City, an African American community on the outskirts of nearby white, wealthy Sausalito.

They, like us, were guarded and wary in those early days, while we all tried to sort out where we belonged and who we trusted.

We Bolinas kids had to get up at 5:30 AM to catch the bus. The bus first picked up kids who lived on the Mesa, next stop, Downtown Bolinas, then around the lagoon to Stinson Beach and along the coast to Muir Beach, picking up kids at every stop. Some of the turns on Shoreline Highway were so sharp, the driver had to brake and back up, making two- and three-point turns. Our ride to school took an hour and a half each way.

I sat near the front, away from the dope smokers in the back—Bolinas had a reputation as the worst route a bus driver could get, with kids who disrespected the drivers. In the first month of school, we went through five drivers.

Clarence was our sixth. He was a tall, mellow man with a large Afro and mirrored sunglasses. His first day, the dope smokers talked him into stopping at Ed's Superette market in Stinson Beach for junk food. After that, this stop became ritual. Clarence stopped the bus, and we all ran out and up the short, steep hill to Ed's Superette.

"Ten minutes," Clarence called. "Thanks, Clarence," we said and gorged on candy, potato chips, pepperoni sticks, and sodas on the rest of the ride home, foods forbidden by our hippy parents.

After school I was riding my horse and saw the bus parked by Agate Beach. Clarence and the potheads were smoking a joint in the front of the bus. The radio was play-ing, and they were laughing.

When I boarded the bus the next morning, I grinned at Clarence. "How was the beach?"

He grinned back. "It was good, Becky. Just remember who lets you go to Ed's."

"We're cool, Clarence," I said.

OUR FRESHMAN DRAMA production was *The Hobbit*. I played Thorin Oakenshield, king of the dwarves, wearing body padding and a beard and mustache. I had a glow-in-the-dark sword with which I slew goblins and a dragon.

After opening night, Mom sat rooted to her chair. "When you walked onstage, for a moment, I thought you were your father."

IN THE LOCKER room, a girl named Sheila said, "You're from Bolinas, right?" We both had big boobs, and we hurried to get into our gym clothes, not wanting anyone to see us na-ked. A week later, she asked me if I wanted to try a little cocaine. We were standing behind the bleachers in our gym shorts and reversible red and blue Physical Education shirts.

"C'mon," Sheila said. "It'll make your soccer game better."

I nodded. "Okay."

She took out a small mirror, a razor blade, and a tiny white envelope and set them on the bleacher. She carefully tapped the coke onto the mirror and cut it into four lines. Then she rolled up a dollar bill, plugged one nostril with her finger, and carefully snorted a line.

"Hold your breath," she said. "Don't blow the coke away."

I took the bill and inhaled. Copying her, I rubbed my finger across the mirror and rubbed the leftover dust into my gums.

The boys burst out of their side of the locker room. "Everyone on the field," the PE teacher said.

I had the ball and was traveling carefully when the coke kicked in. A boy named Pete Hanson closed in on me. He weighed about two hundred pounds and had short and stubby legs, but he was fast.

"Watch this," he called to the other boys. "I'm gonna grab her tit."

It was how the boys won: When a girl was trying to kick a goal, they'd grab at her and distract her from the shot.

My heart surged, and my chest seemed to crack wide open. Pete gained on me and reached for my boob. I body-slammed him right at the hip, and he landed flat on his ass. The goalie came out of the box and raised his hands, but I shot the ball up over his head, scoring a goal.

I ate mushrooms, too, with Crystal, a stray teenager my mother brought home and briefly adopted. Crystal was fifteen, and her parents had simply disappeared. Nobody talked about it, but we all knew her father was running from the FBI. Behind Crystal's back, people said he had buried large amounts of cocaine somewhere in the Arizona desert.

"Don't ask Crystal about her father," my mother warned. "You'll upset her, she's not responsible for him."

My mother took us to the Gay Pride Parade in San Francisco.

"Why are we going?" I asked. "We're not gay."

"We march in support of freedom for all people, we march for civil and human rights." My mother wore a red T-shirt that read LADIES SEWING CIRCLE AND TERRORIST SOCIETY, and she carried a sign that said MY SEXUALITY IS MY BUSINESS. Crystal and I carried matching signs that read KEEP YOUR LAWS OFF MY BODY. We marched with Dykes on Bikes, drag queens, and half-naked men—a carnival of wildness and joy, and we were *exhilarated*.

Crystal's father had left her a tan Ford Galaxie 500. It was Crystal who taught me to drive. We put the car in neutral, floored it, and shifted into drive to see who could leave the longest skid marks. It was her older brother who gave her the mushrooms when he passed through town.

We ate the mushrooms on a Saturday morning and hiked out Tennessee Valley to the beach, everything becoming more intense and bright as we walked: There were red-winged blackbirds, night-black crows, and white seagulls, their cries sharp and loud. We knew about Carlos Castaneda, Don Juan, and power animals. We decided the birds were our spirit guides.

"It's working," Crystal said.

We held hands and peered into the lace of the leaves around us.

"It's a pattern of the whole world," I said.

We ran along the shore. The waves pulled against my feet, splashing my jeans, and then slid back, making a sucking sound as the water ran out through the rocks and sand. We let go hands, laughing and running in opposite directions.

"I am free," I sang to myself, dancing for the glittering, whispering waves. I crossed a sandbar, danced into a small cove. Suddenly the water pulled hard at my ankles and I staggered.

Crystal shouted, "Run! The tide is coming in."

I was inside the cove, behind a rock fall—the bar of sand I'd crossed had almost disappeared. Crystal was on the other side, far up the beach, standing on dry sand. I backed up against the cliff, my palms extended, trying to ward off the now hissing, black waves.

I thought I'd be sucked out into one of the riptides Mom always warned us about. My brother taught me to count the waves. *Every seventh wave is the biggest*, I remembered. *Go after the seventh*.

A wave caught me, I fell, I got up, counted, then ran hard to Crystal.

"I thought you were dead," she said.

"I could see you, on the other side," I said. "You were life—I was death."

I started vomiting on the ride home. I was in the bathroom when my mother banged on the door.

"Are you sick?"

"Go away. I ate something that made me sick."

"Bullshit, what kind of drugs did you take?"

"Mushrooms, okay? It was awful. I almost died."

"Do you know what's happening to you? Mushrooms are poison, and the poison makes you hallucinate.

"You're having a bad trip," she said through the door. "If you're going to take drugs, you need to know what you're getting yourself into. You've poisoned your system, throw up as much as you can. Throw up, Becky. Do you understand me?"

"Go *away*," I said.

After that, we had a tacit agreement about drugs—I wouldn't tell and she wouldn't ask.

11 · SHE HAD YOU

RUBY, KARA, AND I debated losing our virginity. I was fourteen, and they were both fifteen. Who should we give it to? What would it feel like? Would we get bad reputations? We agreed we would not tell our mothers, no matter what.

Ruby was the first. She was smart: She slept with a guy from out of town so that no one in Bolinas, except Kara and me, would ever know. She called us to come over one Sunday morning.

We went into her room and locked the door. She perched on the edge of her bed, and Kara and I sat on the floor. In a hushed voice, she told us about Fleetwood Mac playing in the background, the bottle of wine, the black light posters, and—finally—sex. She told us everything they did.

"It only hurt a little," Ruby said. "I liked the making out part best, you know—before."

"Would you do it again?" I asked.

"I don't know," Ruby shrugged. "If I feel like it—it's not such a big deal. I just wanted to get it over with."

"Who am I going to do it with?" I said. "Nobody will ask me out. They're all scared of my brother—they think he'll beat them up."

Later, Kara and I bought matching silver bracelets and made a vow to throw them into the ocean when we lost our virginity.

Her boyfriend was a senior and a minor dope dealer. Before their dates, he made his rounds Downtown, talking to his customers and exchanging Baggies for cash. He had a bumper sticker on his car that read ASS, CASH, GAS OR GRASS, NOBODY RIDES FOR FREE.

Kara's mother was furious. She complained to my mother.

"How can she date a dope dealer?" her mother said. "I forbid it, but she won't listen."

My mother said, "If you forbid it, the whole thing might last longer—better to ignore it."

Finally, someone named Tony at Tam High asked me for a date. He was shorter and skinnier than I was. He chain-smoked Winstons, played the drums, and drove a silver Mustang convertible that he was forever fixing in Auto Shop. Best of all, he lived in Mill Valley, over the hill.

We made out in the backseat of his car, and I felt his hardness through his jeans and was surprised by the wetness my body made in response. But going all the way was

different. Tony said he had already done it with his old girlfriend. I said no.

Until he told me he had cancer.

"Look," he said, showing me the red, scaly patches on
his legs and arms. "It's cancer. I'm not supposed to live past
twenty-five. *Please* sleep with me," he said.

On the night we picked to do it, I was really nervous.
Tony's father was out of town. He bought beer, and we had
the house to ourselves.

"Don't get me pregnant," I said, sitting on the edge of
the bed, clutching at the coverlet.

"Don't worry," he said, turning off the light. "I've done
this before."

When we got into bed, we kissed for a while, and then
Tony rolled over on his side. He fumbled with a condom
wrapper.

"You want to help me put this on?" he asked over his
shoulder.

"No," I said, staring up at the ceiling and clenching and
unclenching my fists.

"Okay," he said and rolled back over and on top of me.

There was a flash of pain as he pushed himself into me,
and then he was rocking back and forth.

He grunted, rolled off me, and lay still.

"Did you like it?" Tony asked, as we lay not touching.

"Sure," I lied. *What's to like*, I thought.

"It gets better with practice," he said. "Maybe we can try it again sometime."

"Okay."

I broke up with Tony the next day.

Ruby, Kara, and I decided that, because I didn't enjoy it, my experience with Tony didn't count—I was still a virgin. That Saturday night, we went Downtown to hang out and wait for the start of the dance at the Community Center. We were hoping someone over twenty-one would buy us beer. Willie, a redneck who lived up on Horseshoe Hill, had parked his new truck by the bar. He had both doors open and was blasting "Rock Around the Clock" on his eight-track player. We'd heard that the night before there'd been a fight at Smiley's between the rednecks and the Hells Angels. The Bolinas Border Patrol got involved, and someone fired a rifle into the air. We were excited, half-hoping something dramatic would happen again.

"Who do you think you are, the Fonz?" we called to Willie. "Can't you play Bob Marley instead?"

At the dance, we leaned against the wall and watched everyone. Some couples danced together, a loose swing dance; others free-styled facing each other, showing off their moves; a pack of girls danced, tossing their hair, pretending to ignore the boys; other people danced alone, their heads thrown back, arms out, spinning like dervishes.

I spotted Joshua across the room. He was a handsome, blond thirty-six-year-old surfer who looked completely stoned as he bobbed his head to the music. I slipped outside and plucked a bright orange nasturtium out of a flower box near the front door and tucked it behind my ear. I snaked my way across the dance floor toward him.

"Hi," I said. "You wanna dance?"

"Ah, Becky," he smiled, looking down the front of my dress. "You're all grown up."

"Yep," I said.

We danced and danced. When the dance ended, I led him outside and kissed him.

"You're so soft," he murmured. "Will you come home with me?" We drove in Joshua's Datsun to his house, a converted garage crowded with surfboards and wet suits. We climbed into his unmade bed.

"Sweet, sweet," he said as he pulled my clothes off. "You are so sweet."

He had the wide shoulders and lean, smooth muscles of a surfer and a wet suit tan, golden chest and white legs, white butt. He kissed me and stroked my breasts, my belly. Then he parted my legs, slid down, his face between my thighs, opening my pussy with his mouth and tongue, sliding his fingers inside me. He sat up, took my hand, and put it on his hard cock, showing me how to touch him. Then he stroked himself, slid into me gently, smiled, began to move. Suddenly he pulled out of me and came all over my stomach.

"Sorry," he said sheepishly.

After we made love again, he fell asleep, and I lay awake, smiling. Just before dawn I slipped out and ran to the cliff over the beach. As the sun rose, I flung my bracelet into the water. I walked home, hugging myself. I repeated his words, "Becky, you're so sweet." And even though I knew it was trite to think so, I thought of it this way: *I have become a woman.*

My mother was pacing back and forth on the deck when I got home.

"Who do you think you are, young lady?" she said, "sleeping with a thirty-six-year-old man?"

I stared at her. "How did you know?"

"I know everything about you—you're my daughter—you're just a kid."

"I am not," I said. "I'm fourteen. You're the one who made me take a birth control class when I was eleven. Did you think I wasn't going to do it?"

"Not with someone who's old enough to be your father."

She sent Lee to talk to Joshua, who did not come near me again. The next week she took me to Planned Parenthood for a diaphragm.

We did not speak on the way there, and after my appointment, she said, "If you're going to do it, do it with style." We drove to Macy's, where she bought me lingerie.

She selected panties and bras and passed them to me in the dressing room.

"These are for my daughter," I heard her say to the clerk. "She's sexually active now."

"I hate you," I yelled through the door, then heard my mother laugh.

After that, it was war. My mother maintained an injured silence on the subject of sex as I went completely boy crazy. One night, a boy named Sean waited for me in the driveway. We had known each other since we were eight. I used to ride Shaheia past his house, sometimes two or three times, hoping to see him, but when he'd come out, I'd gallop away. Now, we were both fifteen. We'd been hanging out Downtown, flirting, and he'd finally asked me out. When he came to pick me up, he was already stoned on magic mushrooms, but I didn't care.

"Mom," I said. "I'm going out."

My mother was sitting on the edge of her bed, painting her toenails. I stood in her doorway. "Did you hear me?"

"Can't you see I'm busy?" she said.

I was halfway down the deck when she opened the upstairs window and called, "DO YOU HAVE YOUR DIAPHRAGM?"

Horrified, I looked at Sean. He was standing in the street in front of our house, mouth open. He swayed, sank to his knees.

I heard my mom laugh and slam the window shut.

SOMETIMES I STILL tried to please my mother and would make placards that read DON'T BUY NON-UNION GRAPES.

SUPPORT THE FARM WORKERS. I left them in the grape display at Safeway across from Tam High, but then I was caught by an undercover security officer and banned from the store.

I joined the Women's Union at school and was sent as a delegate to the National Women's Conference in Houston, Texas, where I got into an argument with Phyllis Schlafly about the Equal Rights Amendment.

I even talked about joining the Communist Party.

"You don't want to do that," Mom said. "You'd find it too restrictive."

"But I thought you and Dad were communists."

"I was—your father wasn't, really," she said and smiled a little. "He was too much of an independent thinker—mostly, he liked to come to meetings just to stir shit up."

My parents broke from the American Communist Party when they discovered its leadership knew of the atrocities Stalin had committed in the Soviet Union but chose not to disclose his crimes to American Party members. When the truth came out, my parents quit the Party.

"How could we believe in a party that could do such terrible things, then cover them up?" she said.

It was just the two of us in our house again, as Lee had moved to Hawaii with his new girlfriend, Jasmine, a tall, model-beautiful Australian blond he'd met in Bali. They'd had a beautiful baby boy. Lee invited me to come live with them for the summer and take care of the baby.

I went—it was a terrible summer. Lee and Jasmine fought. Once, when he was ranting, she threw a fork at him and impaled it in his foot. I grabbed the baby and ran.

"It's going to be okay," I told the baby. "You'll be okay."

When I was cleaning under Lee and Jasmine's bed, I found guns. I panicked, and my vision went black. Who was he going to shoot? Or would he cause people to shoot him, and then us?

I finally asked Jasmine, and she said they were our dad's hunting rifles. I was scared for Lee. Every night he slept on top of Dad's guns; Dad was killed by guns. When did my brother rest?

WHEN I CAME home from Hawaii, Mom told me Puppers had been hit by a car and killed.

"Where is she buried?" I asked.

She took my hands. "She's not," she said sadly.

Puppers was hit by Cokehead Mike, the stepfather of a kid my age named Bobby. Bobby's mother, Maria, was crazy. The cops were often at their house. A couple of times they tried to take Bobby and his sister and brothers away. Sometimes they'd go to foster homes for a while, but Maria always got them back. In grade school, we did not tease Bobby or his brothers and sister when they came late to school or when they showed up with their heads shaved for lice.

"Mike was high when he hit her," Mom said. "He claimed he didn't see her, she was kind of deaf. He tried to put her out of her pain."

"What are you talking about?"

Mom closed her eyes for moment. "When he hit her, she didn't die, so he backed over her, but she still didn't die, so he backed up and drove over her again, then he took her body to the dump."

I burst into tears, and Mom hugged me hard. "It's a horrible way to die, but Puppers lived twelve years and had a great life. Twelve years! That's a long time for a dog—and she had you, Becky—she had *you*."

IT WAS AFTER Puppers died that Mom started talking about leaving Bolinas. She wanted to sell our house, to take the money and move. Lee wanted her to help him buy some property in Hawaii where he'd build a house for all of us.

"We could live in Hawaii. What do you think of that?" Mom said.

"I think it's a bad idea," I said. "A *very* bad idea."

She conceded, but she did sell the house and loaned Lee most of the money. Leaving Bolinas meant I had to sell Shaheia. Mom was restless, and she didn't really know where she wanted us to go, but she knew that wherever that was, I couldn't bring my horse.

Only one person answered our ad for Shaheia, a rancher from Point Reyes. "I'm looking for a steady horse for my father," he said. "He's getting on in years and he needs a nice horse he can ride to check the fences. Is your mare steady enough?"

"Yes," I said, "she is. She's a good mare."

"How about if I come down tomorrow and bring my trailer with me? If she looks good, I'll just take her back with me, if that's all right with you."

The next day, after checking Shaheia's teeth and her legs for soundness, the rancher said he would take her. My heart sank. Mother prodded me as he finished loading Shaheia into the trailer. "Go on. Just ask him. Go on."

"Excuse me," I said. "Sir, do you think I could come with you? I'd like to see where she's going to be, I'd like to say goodbye."

"Sure." He smiled. "Why don't you follow me? It's a nice place for her, you'll see."

When we got there, I led Shaheia away for a last walk. When we were out of sight of the barn, I jumped up on her bare back. I leaned into her neck and cried. I sang, "Oh, Shaheia, now don't you cry for me."

She chuffed softly and bobbed her head. "I love you," I said. "Please forgive me."

FOR THE NEXT six months, we moved around. First we house-sat in Sausalito for old Party friends, then we lived in two rooms we rented from a single mom with two children. It was in that house that Mom learned she was sick.

I surprised her one night. Her bedroom door was ajar, and she was sitting topless in front of her dressing table mirror, cupping her breasts gently and examining them. They looked angry and swollen. The veins showing through the thin, translucent skin were blue. My mother lifted her head and saw me in the mirror.

"Come in, Becky. There's something I need to talk to you about," she said. "Something's wrong with me. I think I'm sick."

She said six months earlier, her left breast had become inflamed, and she'd gone to see a doctor at UCSF Medical Center. The doctor had diagnosed her with mastitis, a common type of breast infection, and given antibiotics to treat it. She'd asked the doctor to biopsy her breast, but he said no, told her not to worry.

"Now my right breast is inflamed, too. I'm going to have a biopsy on Friday at UCSF hospital in the City. Amalia will come and pick us up, okay?"

I swallowed hard and opened my mouth, but nothing came out.

She nodded. "Go to bed, Becky. It's okay. We just have to wait until Friday."

On Friday, Amalia and I sat in the waiting room at UCSF. A nurse came down the hallway, pushing a scrawny man with no hair in a wheelchair.

"No, no, no," he mumbled. "I don't want to."

I tried not to look at his head or the bony knees jutting out of his green hospital gown.

"What if it's cancer?" Amalia said.

I shook my head. "Let's go find her," I said and stood up.

We pushed open the door of the biopsy room. Mom was sitting in front of a small, stainless steel table. Her breasts were propped up on it. A huge needle stuck out of her right breast. Tears slid down her cheeks, and she was shaking. Behind her stood several doctors and nurses.

"Oh my God," Amalia said. She clutched my shoulders and dug her fingers into me.

A nurse hurried to the door. "You can't be in here, please wait outside."

We went back to the waiting room. I got two Cokes out of the vending machine, and we sat in silence.

Amalia said, "Did Mom ever tell you that story about great-grandma and her inflatable boobs? How she wore them when the minister came for dinner?"

I imitated my mother: "As she set down the turkey in front of your great-grandfather, he jabbed her in the boob with the carving fork . . ."

"There was a great hissing noise as one tit began to deflate," Amalia and I recited together. "*Phhffffhhhhh-hhhhhttt!*"

A bubble of laughter rose up inside me, and I snorted Coke out of my nose.

Amalia laughed, and in unison, we said the tagline to the story: "That'll teach her."

We fell quiet.

"It kinda looked like that, didn't it?" I said.

"Jesus Christ. Yeah, it did," Amalia nodded. "It did."

Later, after the procedure, we found Mom struggling with a nurse and an orderly. "I don't want a wheelchair," she said.

The bandages under her blouse had come loose. A small amount of blood seeped out of the biopsy wound, staining the front of her shirt red. Amalia and I went to her.

"Mom," Amalia said.

"Get me out of here, get me out."

SEVERAL WEEKS LATER, when we got the biopsy results, the doctors spoke to Mom alone. Amalia and I were led into an exam room. Three doctors came in.

"Where is our mother?" Amalia asked.

The oldest doctor answered. "We wanted to speak with you privately before you see her. My name is Dr. Williams," he said, crossing his arms. "I am an oncologist here at UCSF, and these gentlemen are residents in Oncology.

"Your mother has breast cancer," he said.

She had a rare form called "inflammatory," in both breasts and the lymph glands under her arms. It was a "liquid" kind, which meant it could not be cut out, like a tumor. Mom would start radiation therapy immediately to try to stop it.

"I'm sorry," Dr. Williams said. "How old is each of you?"

"Twenty-seven," Amalia said.

"Sixteen," I said.

"As her daughters, you need to understand that your chances of getting breast cancer are now 50 percent greater than women in the general population. This means you are genetically predisposed—do you understand what this means?"

In that moment I became afraid of my body, a fear I would live with for years. I felt marked by my mother's diagnosis, like I was a time bomb waiting to go off.

Amalia and I stared at the doctor. He cleared his throat and handed Amalia several sheets of paper. "This is her schedule for radiation, this is a list of side effects she may exhibit."

We looked at it together: "Profound fatigue, sunburn-like appearance of breast skin, loss of appetite . . ."

"I know this is a lot to take in," the doctor said, "but we need to begin radiation tomorrow, and I want you to prepare yourselves for what comes next—your mother's waiting outside. She wants to go home."

In the elevator I could not look at my mother and I jabbed the CLOSE DOOR button on the elevator repeatedly.

As we rode down, she wept. "Goddammit," she said. "I'm not dead yet."

12 · HOW I'M GONNA LIVE

MY MOTHER'S RADIATION treatments began in early May, in 1979, a month before the end of my junior year in high school. Several weeks into it, she quit after a botched treatment. The technician forgot to put in the blocks that direct the beam and radiated my mom's entire chest. In the fallout afterward, she learned the doctors were advising a double mastectomy for her, but they didn't believe the radiation nor the mastectomy would work. They didn't think she would survive; the cancer was too advanced.

She stopped Western medicine altogether and bought books on laetrile, vitamin C therapy, enzyme therapy, visualization, meditation, and nutrition. She enrolled in a two-week food and cleansing retreat in Santa Cruz, and she came back glowing and thin.

"I lost twenty pounds," she said. "I feel so much better. Becky, you must do this diet, I know it will help you feel better about yourself. Here, let me show you," she said, pulling a small book out of her shoulder bag and opening it.

"This is James, the man who leads the retreats. He had cancer, and now he's healed—they have a treatment plan all worked out for me."

There was a photo documentation of James on this diet over several months. Each picture had a caption that noted his weight loss. Arms at his sides, he faced the camera in a white loincloth, like an Indian yogi. In each successive picture he looked more and more skeletal. In the last photo, I could see his ribs and the bones in his legs.

My mother pulled out a laminated poster, "This," my mother said, "is a food combining chart. From now on, this is how we are going to eat. This is how I'm going to get well."

Using double-sided tape, she slapped the chart on the refrigerator door. With bright colors and arrows, the chart illustrated what vegetables, fruits, and proteins you should (or should not) eat together in order to improve your nutrient absorption as well as your digestion. The accompanying booklet—which my mother read to me over our dinner of unseasoned grilled chicken and steamed beets—explained how humans, as the original hunters and gathers, were not meant to eat more than one or two of the "food groups" at the same time. If we combined fruits, vegetables, and meats all at once, we couldn't process the foods correctly. Disease was the result, or *dis*-ease. Proper food combinations would cleanse the colon and help fight cancer.

We ate bean sprouts, sunflower seeds, almonds, cashews, pumpkin seeds, carrot juice, beet juice, wheatgrass juice, and the tiniest portions of meat. No more cheese, chocolate, bagels, pork chops, spaghetti, milk, coffee, or sugar. We were now living and eating as if we both had cancer.

For the remainder of that summer, my mother rented a house in Brawley, California, near the Mexican border. She had heard that she could easily obtain laetrile, the illegal cancer drug made from apricot pits, in Brawley from Mexican suppliers who crossed over the border almost daily.

She bought a white 1967 Ford Falcon and made me drive her everywhere because driving hurt her arms. That summer, my mom began to shrink. She lost her curvy hips and thighs. Her left breast hung down lower than her right and looked lopsided under her clothes. Her back and shoulders began to curve over as if to hide and protect her breasts from sharp edges, door frames, and sudden, careless elbows.

She had her hair cut close to the scalp because it was too hard to raise her arms to brush it. The cut and the changes in her body made her look dwarfish and deformed. *My Incredible Shrinking Mother*, I'd think. She had trouble with small motor movements, opening jars, washing dishes, and wringing out her washcloth. Most days I had to help her—although she insisted on changing the bandages on her breasts by herself, alone in the bathroom with the door shut.

My mother bought and read all the books she could find about people healing themselves. These books made her cry. When the books didn't help, she found a man who specialized in lymphatic drainage, which, she explained, was a new therapy that Western medicine didn't yet recognize. She was certain it would be central to her getting well.

"If I'm going to get well, I have to be able to get my lymph glands to drain the toxins out of me," she explained. "It would be good for you to clear some toxins out of your body, too," she said.

On Wednesday afternoons, we went for our treatments together. The practitioner was a tall, skinny man named Warren who had big, brooding blue eyes and long, bony fingers. His home office reeked of incense.

Warren asked me, "How old are you?"

"Sixteen."

"How much do you weigh?"

"One twenty-five," I lied.

"With these treatments, you will not only lose toxins, you'll also lose weight. Now, take off your shirt and bra and lie down."

I did, and he dug his fingers into my neck and chest, saying, "This is where we want to open up the drainage system— hmm, sore there? That means your systems are not draining."

My mother and I both had long red lines on our necks and faces as we drove home. "I think this is going to help, I just know it. Don't you think so?"

I gripped the steering wheel tighter. "Yeah, Mom," I said. "Whatever."

When I went for my second treatment, Warren said, "I want you to take off all of your clothes and look at yourself in the mirror."

I did and stood shivering in front of the full-length mirror, my arms crossed awkwardly across my chest, trying not to look at my dark pubic hair.

He stood behind me and placed his hands on my shoulders. "Don't be shy or ashamed," he said. "Drop your arms."

I did.

"See how much weight you've already lost? There's a very beautiful woman in there, waiting to get out," he said, gently stroking my upper arms. "Very beautiful," he murmured, cupping his hands under my breasts and lifting them gently. He flicked his thumbs, once, across my nipples. "A very sexy, beautiful young woman," he smiled at me in the mirror, "just waiting."

"I think these treatments are helping a lot," my mother said afterward, gently touching her neck and chest. "I feel better, don't you?"

The third treatment, I lied and said I didn't feel well and had to skip it. I was waiting for my mother in the Falcon when the front door to Warren's office opened and my mother hurried out barefoot. She was pulling her clothes around her, trying to button her shirt with one hand. She carried her shoes and socks in the other hand, dragging her coat and purse on the ground behind.

"Pervert," she said, dropping a shoe.

Warren ran out the door. "Wait," he said. "I can save you! I know I can."

"Charlatan," my mother said, jerking at the car door handle. "Becky, open this—he came on to me," she said. "He fondled my breasts. What kind of pervert comes on to a woman with breast cancer? If he were a real doctor, I'd report him."

I shoved her coat and purse into the backseat, then ran up the stairs and picked up my mother's shoe and pointed it at Warren.

"Fuck you, creep," I said.

OUR ROLES BEGAN to reverse: She became more dependent, and I, the parent. Over meals, Mother spoke to me in measured tones, adult to adult, as if I were her equal, or even superior to her, the doctor. Sometimes she was like a wife, and I, her husband. I was her guardian, her confidant.

Mom believed if she did everything right, she would heal herself. But if she didn't, she would not get well. These theories were paradoxical and perilous. It was a weird hybrid of faith and denial on one hand, and blame and denial on the other. As each treatment failed, she moved on to the next one, willing herself to believe.

I'd turned seventeen—it was impossible to imagine my life without my mom. She was my only parent; I couldn't imagine her dead. And so we did not talk about the possibility of her dying, and what might happen to me if she did. We both put everything into the belief that she'd get well. This was our pact, our dance, our fragile alliance.

My mother spoke only once of the possibility of her death. She took me to a spiritualist church, where members channeled messages from spirits, or the dead.

A tall woman greeted us at the doorway of the church. "Welcome. Have you come for a healing?"

"Yes," my mother said, while I stared at my feet. "We have."

"Please take a program, it explains today's order of service. After the service, there will be messages for some people. I hope that you will be able to receive what may be given."

"Thank you," my mother said.

The reverend was a stout man, gray-haired, dressed in a black robe and green stole. He prayed, "The light of God surrounds us, the love of God enfolds us, the power of God protects us, and the presence of God watches over us—wherever we are, God is, and all is well, amen.

"And now, we will give healings," he said. "We believe that the spirits are our allies and they can tell of the things we cannot know in our daily lives. Don't be afraid."

People came forward to sit in the healer's chairs. Mom and I joined the line. When Mom was seated, a small, dark-haired woman came to her and said, "You have a question?"

"Yes," Mom said, "I do."

I was leaning over, trying to hear, when someone took my hand and gently pulled me around. A blond woman stood beside me. "Come with me, please." Still holding my hand, she led me away to a pew at the back of the church.

"Sit," she said, smiling. "I have a message for you."

I stopped breathing. *My mom*, I thought.

"Do you play a musical instrument?" the woman asked.

Memories flashed in my mind of the piano built in our house in Bolinas, of Penny and my failed music lessons.

"No," I said to the woman standing beside me in the church, "I don't. You must be thinking of my sister, she's a flautist."

"Perhaps it's something else, not music, but you have a lot of creativity. I see a small, blue spirit on your left shoulder, and it's whispering in your ear. You need to listen to it."

As we drove away, I said, "What did you ask?"

"It's private," my mother replied.

"What does that mean? It's just you and me here. You have to tell me."

She sighed. "I asked if my daughter was going to be all right if—if I don't make it. I didn't even ask about your brother. I was worried about you, but the healer said I had it backward. She said it's my married daughter who's in trouble, that she's trapped in a marriage that's killing her. She said that you're strong, that you're the one who will be fine."

BRAWLEY WAS 611 miles south of Bolinas, 25 miles north of the Mexican Border. Our house in Brawley had a swimming pool. While my mother lay in the back bedroom and listened to Pachelbel, I hung out at the pool and watched the boy next door.

His name was Dennis, and he draped himself over the fence to watch me swim in my new brown bikini with thin orange and yellow stripes, or he invented excuses to come over. He'd ask about my mom, or my high school up north, or how I was going to play first-string goalie on the girls' soccer team that fall, or what it was like to be in Drama class. He would ask me anything, stuttering and blushing, just to be near me.

We had been living on watermelon and wheatgrass for a month and a half when my brother flew from Hawaii to San Diego and then drove to Brawley, saying he'd come to check on Mom. He arrived in the afternoon, when my mother was always at her worst. In the mornings, she could sing along with opera while I sliced up watermelon, but as the day wore on she became sadder and slower. When Lee saw her, his mouth fell open and he all but froze. Then he dropped his eyes, reached into his back pocket, and hurriedly began laying out hundred-dollar bills on the table.

"I gotta fly back tonight, Mom, but here's some money for meds, or whatever you need, more watermelon, whatever. You need anything, you just call. What doctors are you seeing now? What drugs are you taking?"

My mother looks at him blankly. "I'm sorry, you came at a bad time of day, Lee. I need to nap. We can talk when I get up."

"Yeah, okay, Mom, you go rest." When she leaves the room, he turns on me.

"You know why Mom has cancer, don't you? It's from all those years of eating shit like pork chops and candy and drinking that horrible black coffee. She was fat! She never exercised! And look what it got her, and you ate all that shit with her, and look at you, you're fat. You've been living on nothing but watermelon, and you're *still* fat!"

"Shut up," I say, covering my ears.

"You want to end up like Mom? She's fucking dying, man, from all that poison."

"Leave us alone!" I shout. "We're doing *fine.*"

"What's this 'we' shit? Are you her twin now?" He circles me. "Here, for every ten pounds you lose, I'll give you a hundred dollars, okay? Twenty pounds, that's two hundred bucks."

I stand rooted to the floor.

He waves the money in my face. "Take it," he says.

"That's enough, Lee." Our mother stands in the doorway, topless, in blue striped pajama bottoms and bare feet.

Her thin arms hang at her sides, but her eyes are bright with rage. "We don't need you here."

Lee stares open-mouthed at Mom's bare chest, then turns and hurries out of the house. My mother stands in the kitchen, listening to the tires of the rental car squeal as he pulls out of the driveway and speeds away.

"Motherfucker."

That evening, after my mother naps and does her wellness visualizations, we sit in the kitchen, listening to the cicadas. She no longer bothered to put on a shirt.

"Get me my juice, please, Becky."

I open the refrigerator and take out the jar of wheatgrass and set it on the table.

"You know what this cancer is, don't you, Becky? It's my own anger, fear, and rage eating its way through my chest, my grief for your father, for my life. In my visualizations, I see it as the Red Army. I send in the Blue Army to beat it—that's how I'm gonna live. Please pour me some juice, I don't have the strength to open the jar tonight."

She sits quietly for a while.

Then she says, "One of these days you're going to figure out that you are very angry with me."

"No," I say to the floor. "I'm not."

She leans over and touches my hand. "Yes you are."

13 · HEAL YOUR BODY

MY MOTHER RENTED a house in Forest Knolls, where I'd gone to camp as a child. Like Bolinas, Forest Knolls is in west Marin County, but it lies fourteen miles inland, in a narrow valley, shaded by redwoods. The town is split in half by Sir Francis Drake Boulevard, a two-lane curvy road that runs from San Quentin to the edge of the Point Reyes National Seashore. In Forest Knolls, population 465, there was a gas station just down the road and, further on, a bar, a tiny corner grocery store, and a post office. It was the fall of 1979.

Our new house was on the inside of a blind curve in Sir Francis Drake Boulevard. A tall wooden fence obscured it from the road, but on Saturdays and Sundays, we could hear the cars as they sped toward Point Reyes for the weekend. There were no close neighbors. Mom and I didn't know anyone.

"This is *perfect*," my mother said. "I know I can get well here."

But I hated that house. The wet redwood trees dripped onto the roof and onto the plastic trays of wheatgrass growing on the back porch, making a constant *ping, ping, ping*-ing sound. The kitchen was an apothecary of my mother's herbs, vegetables, tonics, balms, and vitamins. On the wall was an erasable board where she tracked the rotation and dosages of what she called her different "medications." A bright yellow vegetable juicer and its attachments stood on the counter. As a reminder to herself to oil the crank of the juicer, my mother had written, *Grease Me, Babe* in indelible red ink along its side. The shelves were lined with her inspirational books. The house smelled of herbs and vitamins and, gradually, the sweet, heavy smell of my mother's illness.

Right after we moved in, I'd had to petition my school principal to let me stay in the same high school, Tam High. As soon as my senior year began, I'd started sleeping with my varsity soccer coach, Bruce Sherman. Bruce was twenty-five years old and a Religious Studies/Sociology major at San Francisco State University. His father was a Presbyterian minister, and after practice, Bruce and I made out in the backseat of his Volkswagen Squareback.

My mother was upset about Bruce. "You're sleeping with a minister's son? I mean, really, Rebecca."

MY MOTHER ATTENDED a workshop called "Co-Counseling: The Therapy without Therapists. Learn to Clear Emotions through the Discharge Process."

"It's based on the idea that we all hold psychological hurts inside," she told me, "and that we can clear away present and ancient traumatic experiences by letting those emotions out. You can even let go of emotions you had before you were born, that are still impacting your life today."

She talked about a woman in the training who could remember being in her mother's womb at eight months, who'd been able to recover a memory of her father making love to her mother, and this sense of invasion had blocked her own sexuality, which was why she'd never had an orgasm.

"Once she was able to discharge the negative emotion, she was able to heal her sexuality," Mom said. "Isn't that amazing?"

She asked me to go with her to the next workshop, and I reluctantly agreed. We sat in the back. Two men named Alex and Antonio were giving the presentation. My mother leaned over to me and whispered, "Antonio's hands are the hands of an artist or a musician, *that's* the kind of man you need."

I whispered back, "I didn't realize we were here to pick up men. And, by the way, he's gay, Mom. In fact, they're *both* gay."

"You don't know that—you need a better boyfriend. Bruce isn't good for you."

Co-counseling sessions required only two people: one to play the role of the "counselor," the other to take the role of the "client." After thirty minutes, you switched. It was the counselor's job to witness the client's discharge of emotion and remain calm and accepting and neutral. The counselor was not allowed to comment on or judge the client's emotions, even if they were about the counselor.

The counselor also had to help the client "get back" if the client went too deeply into a negative memory or emotion and "got lost" in the retelling of the trauma. In the mini practice session, I was instructed to hold the client's hand, make eye contact, and comfort the client by gently saying, "It's all right, let it out, I'm right here."

In the instances where the discharge of a really negative emotion was needed, the counselor could hold a pillow up and let the client hit it while discharging. My mother was convinced that daily sessions would help her clear out all the anger and grief she was "manifesting" in her breasts as cancer. She did minisessions on the phone with people when she felt depressed or sick.

My mother insisted we do at least one session together every week and that I write down "issues" I wanted to work on in my sessions. In my journal, I made a list that included:

Co-counseling Issues
(DO NOT TALK ABOUT WITH MOM!)

Try not to take responsibility for my Mom's life

Dad's death

My temper

Issues That Need a Small Amount of Attention

That I need help and that's okay

That it's okay for me NOT to be sick with cancer

Guilt for being white

In my first session with my mother, I took the role of the counselor first. We sat on the floor on top of pillows.

I held both her hands in mine and said, "What are you feeling right now?"

"I feel sad and guilty. I need to talk about my feelings about your father, I've kept them in for so long. I loved your father, but some little part of me was relieved when he was killed." My mother began to cry. "I know that sounds terrible, but I have to get it out. He was just so fucking difficult to live with—there was so much fear and violence. And he was also *so alive*, like a bright and terrible light. It feels good to say all this out loud. I've never forgiven myself for feeling that, I did love him so much." She wept harder.

"My mother taught me not to love anyone because she never loved me—never. I know you think I don't love you, Becky, but I do. I'm so scared, I don't want to die."

I held a pillow up. "Go on," I said. "Hit it, let out all the sadness."

While she shook and cried and beat on the pillow with one fist, I held her other hand. Her bony fingers made me think of wishbones. Her skin was slightly green and papery, and I felt afraid to squeeze her hands, fearing her fragile bones might snap. My own hands felt huge and clumsy.

After thirty minutes, my mother wiped her eyes and said, "Now it's your turn, Becky. What are you feeling now?"

"I don't feel anything."

"How do you feel about my being sick? Just for the session, pretend I'm not your mother. Go ahead, let it out."

"I can't," I said.

"Talk about the other things you're angry about. Let them lead you."

"I am angry," I said.

"Good, good."

"I'm mad because I—because I fucked up in soccer practice yesterday and let a goal get by me, and I got a B+ instead of an A on my Constitution test, and because I always get the part of the whore in Drama class—there, are you happy? Now, can I please go?"

Whenever I remember co-counseling with my mother, it makes me cringe—I cannot imagine a more fucked-up idea. But at the time, we dressed it up and felt this to be brave, progressive, honest, mature. Co-counseling together made us equals. We believed that in doing this together, we were helping her.

I once met an actual therapist who had worked with my mother. "I remember her clearly," he said. "Very brilliant, very damaged."

I was shocked, not so much by his description, but by the fact that she had sought psychotherapy and hadn't told me. I thought I knew everything about my mother, that I was her confidant, an extension of her, really. This was as she wanted our relationship to be. Because I loved her, I liked it that way, too.

When I got over my shock from hearing about her therapy, I knew he was right. Very brilliant. And very, very damaged. All those deaths, the babies, Dad—and although she said his death liberated her in some way, allowing her to be herself, she was traumatized and never recovered from the shock.

"I JUST CAN'T deal with other people's negative emotions about my cancer, Becky. I only want positive people around me," my mother said. She refused to let anyone in the house unless they were fellow co-counselors or those friends who could make her laugh.

"Unless people can express their feelings about me within the confines of a session, I don't want to hear about it. I must protect myself from their fear."

I'd overhear her on the phone to some concerned friend: "We're fine. I'm in remission right now—no, it's really not a good time to visit. I'll let you know if I need anything. Thanks for calling."

There were only three people my mother would let into the house regularly, Joyce, Stewart, and Annie.

Joyce was a slender, blond nurse practitioner from the medical clinic in Bolinas. After that first birth control class when I was eleven, Joyce had helped my mother lead annual sex education classes for the women and girls in Bolinas.

Stewart was a bearded clarinet player who liked to argue politics and music. When we lived in Bolinas, he'd come over and cook huge meals for us and then he and my mother would argue hotly about how to create change in the world.

Annie was a writer. Her father, a writer too, had developed a brain tumor a year before my mother was diagnosed with breast cancer. When Annie came over to visit my mom, they would sit in the kitchen drinking wine and swapping wild stories, conspiring in whispers and making fun of people they hated. Annie and my mom laughed and laughed and *laughed*.

When Annie's father, Ken, became ill, I'd see her and her younger brother, Steve, out walking with him. Ken had covered his head with a brightly colored crocheted hat. Later, after surgeries, his head was wrapped in white bandages. As he got sicker, he'd forget my name and Annie would prod him gently. "That's Becky, Dad, remember? Barbara's daughter."

He'd smile, nod absently.

"Hi," I'd say. "Nice to see you." But really, I was afraid of him, afraid he would jinx us, that his cancer might be contagious. He died two months after my mother was diagnosed, when I was sixteen. My mom and I went to his memorial service on Mount Tamalpais. She cried through the whole ceremony. I stood next to her, holding her hand, thinking: *This is not going to happen to us.*

I STARTED SNEAKING food into the house. When I went shopping for vitamins and organic vegetables for my mom, I also bought whole salamis and bags of pecan shortbread cookies and hid them in my backpack. I ate all this at night in bed, and in the morning I'd smuggle out the empty packages and wrappers. Driving home from school, I stopped at the 7-Eleven and bought candy bars and bags of potato chips. After I ate, I felt calm, but also ashamed. I simply couldn't seem to stop eating. I was sure that my mother would find out when I started to gain weight. At school, I heard that if you could throw up after eating, you could eat all you wanted to and not get fat.

Often, at night, through the walls, I heard my mother weeping. When she wept, I ate cookies until I felt sick. I'd throw whatever food was left out the window then sneak into the bathroom and stick my finger down my throat and vomit. When she had finally cried herself to sleep, I'd sneak out of the house in my nightgown and crawl through the bushes under my window, searching for the cookies. Hidden in the dark, I'd kneel, filling my mouth with their small, moist sweetness.

MY MOTHER BEGAN to shrink even more rapidly. She had been a tall, full woman at five foot ten. Now even her nose and mouth seemed smaller; the skin over her facial bones grew taunt and shiny. When she swallowed, I could see the enzyme tablet or vitamin and juice traveling down her throat. She had been steadily losing weight on her belly and hips, her thick thighs and the soft, fleshy parts of her upper arms. And then her bones, her limbs, even her head seemed to shrink, while her feet and hands grew elongated and strangely beautiful, the pattern of tendons, muscles, and bones visible, strong, luminous: interconnecting lines that unfailingly flexed and extended as she carefully picked up her small mound of vitamins or walked barefoot to the bathroom.

Glaring at me over her 6:00 AM glass of wheatgrass juice, she'd snarl, "What are you staring at?"

"Nothing," I mumbled.

"Well, knock it off. You're making me feel like a bug, and you know I can't afford to feel bad. I need to do my affirmations, and I have a new one to show you."

She handed me a book entitled *Heal Your Body*, by Louise L. Hay.

I opened the book to the page she had marked.

Problem: Cancer

*Probable Cause: Deep hurt. Longstanding
resentment. Deep secret or grief eating away at the
self. Carrying hatreds. "What's the use?"*

*New Thought Pattern: I lovingly forgive myself
and release all of the past. I choose to fill my world
with joy. I love and approve of myself.*

"I just have to start *really* loving myself, Becky. You, too. Come here," she said and led me into the bathroom.

"What, now, Mom?"

"I want you to look at yourself in the mirror. Go on, now say, 'I love you' to yourself."

"I don't want to—Mom, you know I *hate* this kind of thing."

"Try it just once. I'll leave so you can have some privacy," she said and softly closed the door.

I tried to look at myself in the mirror, but my eyes kept sliding off the image of my face.

"Doesn't it feel good?" my mother called through the door.

"Go away and I'll do it." I took a deep breath, and for an instant, I looked myself in the eyes. "I love you," I whispered, then burst into tears.

Later that night, when I think my mother is asleep, I creep toward the bathroom. The door is open, and the light on. My mother stands naked in front of the medicine cabinet mirror, sponging the oatmeal poultice off her breasts with a washcloth. She does the poultices twice a day. She tries to do it when I'm not home to see it, but I know anyway.

When I do the laundry, the fronts of her shirts are often damp with fluid. I pick her shirts up at the edges, trying not to touch them or get the sweet, rancid stink on my hands. If I do, I can't seem to wash it off completely, and it lingers on my skin, like mildew, for days.

Now, her right breast has shrunk into a hard-looking lump. As I watch, she reaches up and gently pokes at it with her index finger, but the flesh doesn't move. It's like a clean, hard, shiny, dark scab stuck on the front of her chest, like something alien or glued on that doesn't belong to her human body.

"That's good," I hear her tell herself as she gently squeezes the nipple. "At least it's not draining anymore."

In contrast, her left breast hangs low, swollen and bloated looking. The blue veins stand out in the red and angry flesh. Her left nipple has scabs, or bits of oatmeal stuck to it; from where I'm standing, I can't tell which. But then she touches one place on her nipple and a scab breaks open and a little yellow fluid seeps out. "Shit," she says, reaching for the washcloth at the edge of the basin, delicately blotting her breast.

I shove the sleeve of my nightgown into my mouth and bite down hard, step further back into the darkness.

She picks up a piece of aloe vera plant from the top of the toilet water-tank. The thick outer skin of the plant has been slit open. She carefully wipes the clear juice onto her hand and spreads it across her right breast and then more delicately on the left.

She tries to practice a gentle version of *lomi lomi* on herself, a Hawaiian form of massage, using aloe vera as a lubricant.

"Let there be love," she intones softly as she spreads the gel across her chest. "Let there be power / Let there be harmony / Let there be healing . . ." Then she murmurs to herself in the mirror, "I love you, I love you, I love you."

The aloe vera makes her breasts look shinier. She pulls on a white sleeveless undershirt and then, for warmth, a soft, baggy long john shirt. She stares at herself again in the mirror. She opens her mouth and sticks her jaw out toward her reflection, her expression exactly as it's always been just before she'd apply her lipstick.

Suddenly, she bares her teeth at the mirror to say, "Well, you're not dead yet."

14 · TOO LATE

IN OUR SENIOR Drama class, we were getting ready for college auditions. Everyone who planned to audition for Juilliard or NYU had to prepare two five-minute monologues: one from a modern play and one Shakespearean, one comic and one tragic. We were to perform our monologues at the senior drama night. Each of us had to meet with the Drama teacher privately to discuss how we planned to prepare and rehearse the material.

Our teacher, Mr. Caldwell, was nationally known, and because of his reputation, Tam High's Drama department was rated as one of the best in the country. Several of his students had become Broadway actors and movie stars, including Kathleen Quinlan and Merritt Butrick. We all were afraid of him, in awe of him. Each of us wanted to be his next success story.

"I only have one piece," I said.

"You need two if you want to audition."

"I can't think about college right now, my mom's too sick."

He cleared his throat. "Yes, I know," he said, his voice deep. "And I'm sorry."

"But I want to do one monologue at the senior drama night, if you'll let me."

"Which piece?"

"It's from *Mourning Pictures* by Honor Moore, a new feminist playwright. It's about her mother having cancer, my Women's History teacher told me about it."

"Are you sure you want to do this in front of an audience? It may be too close to your own experience for you to be able to perform it well, if at all."

"I want to," I said.

He nodded, "Okay, you can try it."

At home, my mother said, "How did your meeting go with your Drama teacher?" She rarely asked about school, but she always asked about Drama class.

"I'm only doing one piece, Mom."

"Well, I want to come, but nights are hard for me. We'll see."

"Okay," I said and pushed myself away from the table. "I gotta go, I have soccer practice, then I have to go to work. I'll be home after midnight."

On Friday and Saturday nights, I had a job washing dishes at a restaurant in Tiburon. Tiburon and Belvedere were where the rich people lived, where the tourists came to eat in restaurants and cafés with views across the Bay of San Francisco.

I'd drive my mother's Ford Falcon to Sam's Anchor Café, where I'd sort, rinse, and load the dirty silverware, bowls, and plates into the dishwasher, then stack them while they were still hot. I carried towers of the clean plates and bowls over to the serving line, where waiters shouted orders at the cooks. When the shift was over, the waiters and cooks smoked dope out on the balcony and then drank in the empty dining room. We ate before our shifts—dishwashers were allowed to eat only hamburgers. At home, I ate what my mother ate and had stopped hiding food in the house because I was so afraid she would find it. At the restaurant, I ate as much as I possibly could. But if employees were caught consuming anything expensive—shrimp cocktail, avocados, fresh crab or fish—they'd be fired. The head chef liked me, though. He chain-smoked on the line and wore his long blond hair in a ponytail that hung halfway down his back. The busboys said he snorted coke with the managers. They said Georgie got away with murder.

One Friday night, Georgie said, "Becky, what kind of fish do you like?"

"Sole. I like sole."

"Okay, kiddo, you got it."

At the end of the shift, Georgie made me a plate of petrale sole, sautéed in egg batter, Dore-style. He stood in the doorway, smoking, while I crouched over the plate and shoveled the hot, salty, buttery fish and rice pilaf into my mouth.

"You know," he said, "you're too good for this place. You should get out of here." He blew smoke out of his nose and glanced over his shoulder. "The guys who wash dishes here are getting paid way more than you are, and that's because you're a girl." He dropped his cigarette on the floor and ground it out. "Besides, everyone who works here is a creep," he smiled. "Except me."

I'd always stop at Zim's restaurant on the way home and order french fries and a chocolate shake. I sat alone in a corner booth, sweaty and smelling of dirty dishes, cleanser, and garbage.

Even though I was sticking my finger down my throat after eating to throw up, I continued to gain weight.

"I don't understand it," my mother said. "You should be losing weight."

I read an article in a women's fashion magazine about female runners who wrapped their bodies in Saran wrap before working out to lose weight faster. Before soccer practice I hid in the bathroom stall in the women's locker room, stripped down to my underpants, and then wrapped myself in Saran wrap from my chest to my butt.

In the same magazine, I'd read about losing weight with appetite suppressants, like Ayds candy and Dexatrim, and laxatives. I started buying Dexatrim and chocolate-flavored Ex-Lax at 7-Eleven stores, changing stores when the clerks started to recognize me. I was taking Dexatrim during the day, but by the time I got to work, it had worn off and I gorged myself. Afterward, each night before bed, I ate four squares of Ex-Lax.

When I got home from Sam's that night, I opened the door without turning on the light and crept into the bathroom to try to wash the smell of fries and chocolate off me.

"Becky, is that you?" Mom called out from her bedroom before I had washed. "How was work? Come and say good night."

I went and stood in the doorway, hoping she couldn't smell the greasy food from her bed. Stewart had come to visit, and he was sitting by her with a book in his hands. Years later, he'd tell me he'd been in love with her.

She sniffed the air. "You smell like dope and fried food. Are you smoking a lot of pot? Pot will just make you crave fatty food, and fried foods are bad for you."

"It's the smell of the restaurant," I said. "Everybody there smokes pot, too—don't worry, I'm not taking drugs."

I did not tell my mother about getting paid less than the boys. I knew it would make her furious, but I was angry about it and decided to quit. I drove to Sam's the next morning. When I met with the manager, I was too scared to say what I'd learned. Instead, I said, "My mom has cancer, I have to quit."

MOM FELT WELL enough to come to the senior drama night—something I hadn't planned on. By then, she knew what I was performing—it was too late to change it, but I cut out parts I thought would upset her.

She carefully made up her face with organic Indian Earth makeup, which came in a little clay pot with a cork top. She applied the reddish powder with a paintbrush to her cheeks and chin, as she did every day. "It makes me feel better," she said.

The cancer had spread to her liver, which released toxins that caused her skin to turn yellow-green. The Indian Earth helped to mask it. In the daytime, she sometimes put on too much and looked a little clownish, as if she were wearing too much brown stage makeup. But that night, she looked elegant, angular, her haughty self again.

My mother always put on lipstick before she went out of the house. She'd done this for as long as I could remember. And before she'd get out of the car, she'd touch it up in the rearview mirror, blotting her lips on whatever paper she had at hand: an envelope, the back of a bank statement, a bill, a napkin saved from a restaurant for just that purpose, a ratty, old piece of Kleenex.

That night, she applied red lipstick and carefully blotted her lips on a single square of toilet paper.

Smiling into the rearview mirror, she said, "I always feel better when I get dressed up." She had on a bright scarf around her short hair and a loose coat to hide her chest. "We need to get there early, Becky. I cannot be jostled."

"I know. I saved you a seat in the back row, where you'll be safe."

Onstage I recited, "I can't see myself. How do I know I'm me and not her? . . . I have always been her, and it's never mattered before who was who . . . How do I know I won't have pain, as much as she does, when I move?"

I advanced a step.

"I see you," I whispered over the audience toward the dark shape of my mother, huddled in the back row. "I love you. I don't want to die."

In the car, my mother was very quiet.

"Mom, *please*," I said. "Say something."

"That was *very* brave, Becky," she said. "I'm *very* proud of you."

TWO NIGHTS LATER when I got home from a date with Bruce, our driveway was filled with flashing red lights and incoherent radio-transmitted voices. An ambulance driver was wheeling my mother on a gurney.

I ran toward them. "Mom? Are you okay, Mom?"

The ambulance driver turned to face me. It was Al, the bus driver from Bolinas School. He was crying.

My fault, I thought automatically. *It was my monologue—it made her sick. I didn't mean to hurt her.*

"What are you doing here? What's happened?" I cried.

"I'm an emergency techie now, an EMT," Al said. "When I got the call, I had no idea it was your mother,

Becky. She's had a crisis, but she tried to wait until you got home. She wants you to follow us to the emergency room. She's in a lot of pain—she's very, very sick," he said.

They loaded her into the ambulance. I tried to see through the swinging IV lines of plasma and morphine, but she had turned her face away.

I followed the ambulance in the Falcon. In the emergency room, my mother was immediately fighting with the doctor.

"I don't want to be admitted. I was just having trouble breathing—it's the pain. Just give me something for it, something to take home."

"But you need to be in the hospital, you need help," he argued. "I can't help you unless you admit yourself."

"I know what I need," she said, her voice rising. "If you won't help me, I'll find someone who will. Becky, go get the car."

I drove us home into the dark valley. It was raining, and my mother was crying. Her cancer had metastasized and was now in her brain. She had moments of lucidity, then moments of true madness.

All that remained constant was her adamant denial.

A FEW DAYS later she got a letter that made her very happy. "I want to share something amazing with you," she said. She reached carefully under her pillow and pulled out an envelope and handed it to me. The envelope was addressed to our Bolinas house and had been forwarded to our house in Forest Knolls. It was from a boy she had known when she was eighteen—Yoshi Sekino—who, with his family, had been taken away to an internment camp during the war. Mom had gone to see him off, the only person in town who did.

"I have always wanted to thank you," he wrote. "I remember watching you through the window: You were wearing a green dress."

"Isn't that wonderful?" she smiled. "After all these years, writing to say *thank you*. When I'm a little stronger, I want to meet him for lunch."

Two weeks later we flew to Leavenworth, Washington, to see another alternative doctor. I drove the rental car slowly, through a snowstorm, trying to see the road.

The lights were on in the doctor's house, and he answered the door immediately.

"Barbara Wilson? I'm Dr. Paul, please come in. I hope you didn't have too much trouble getting here. I hate to be abrupt, but we should get started. I'll need you to undress completely. Your daughter can wait in the living room while I examine you."

I pretended to look at the books in his library. From the other room, I heard the sounds of my mother taking off her clothes. She grunted softly as she climbed onto the examining table.

"Oh, my God," Dr. Paul said.

I peered into the examining room. My mother was hunched up on the table. She had pulled her knees up toward her chest. Under the harsh light of the lamp beside the table, her skin looked very green. She grabbed at the sheet on the table, trying to cover herself back up.

"Why did you wait so long?" Dr. Paul said, waving his hands. "It's too late—I can't help you, Mrs. Wilson—you're dying."

"No," she said. "You have no right to say that. Becky, help me get dressed."

That night we lay in the same double bed in a rickety hotel. I carefully wrapped myself around my mother, my chest against her back, my legs curled against hers. I stroked her head.

"Why can't he help me?" she cried. "Why can't someone help me?"

I awoke during the night. Mother's breathing was ragged, and her breath smelled bad. Underneath her ribs, I felt her heart beating against my chest. The mattress sagged, so we'd each slid into the middle of the bed. Carefully, I moved away from her and crawled out. I put on my socks and shoes and pulled on my coat. I closed the room door quietly and walked quickly to the lobby and out the front door.

The empty streets and buildings glowed a perfect white. I started running. I sobbed and ran, past the dark shops, the buried cars. Snow fell. *She's dying*, I thought, *my mother's actually dying.*

I ran until I could not breathe or feel the ground. Tripping, I fell on my face. I beat my hands against the sidewalk and wept, "Goddammit, God help, help me, God."

AT THE AIRPORT the next morning, Mother asked for a wheelchair. She'd run out of Kleenex and made me steal a roll of toilet paper out of the ladies' room. She tucked it next to her in the wheelchair, beside her pillbox. As we neared the escalator, I thought, *I can end this right now*, as I fantasized pushing her off the escalator, I saw her flying through the air, over the heads of the startled skycaps, the roll of toilet paper unfurling like a banner, the pillbox open, scattering pills as she landed on the luggage carousel, headfirst.

"Becky, slow down," my mother said. "What's the matter with you?"

We got home. I snuck out the next day to call my sister from the pay phone at the gas station while Mom was napping.

"Amalia, you have to come," I said. "You have to help me with Mom."

"I can't," she said firmly.

"You have to!" I yelled into the phone.

That's when I learned my mother had barred her from the house. Amalia had driven down from Santa Rosa to see her, but our mother refused to open the door.

A truck sped down the road, shaking the ground and rumbling the phone booth. "You have to," I whispered, smacking the glass door softly. "Please."

She came.

Amalia's face was bloodless when she walked out of our mother's dark room. The double bed had been replaced with a hospital bed that Mom could raise and lower by herself. I'd covered the windows with white sheets and put twenty-watt bulbs in all the fixtures, because bright lights hurt her eyes.

Amalia and I stood in the kitchen, arguing in whispers. She said, "You can't stay here, this is crazy—you should have told me."

"I did tell you. I've been taking care of Mom for an entire year by myself; I am only *seventeen years old.*"

"Keep your voice down—Mom says she has some friends who are helping her, is that true?"

I nodded. "Yes, Joyce, Stewart, and Annie, but I'm not leaving."

"You must," Amalia said. "You're coming to stay with the kids and me."

"No, I won't go."

She pointed her finger at me. "You have two days to figure something else out. If you can't find somewhere else to stay, then you're coming with me. Mom agrees, ask her yourself."

My mother was drowsing when I crept into her room. She woke and smiled at me. "Come sit," she said, patting the bed beside her. "You need to stay somewhere else for a while. Don't worry, Becky—it's only temporary, just until I get a little stronger."

"Okay," I said.

She leaned toward me and whispered conspiratorially: "Don't believe them, Becky. I'm not dying, it's just a recession. I know you're going to graduate soon." She smiled. "I'm going to be there." She fell asleep holding my hand.

Before she was ill, Mother threatened me. "On your eighteenth birthday, I'm kicking you out, and you'll have to learn to be on your own, like I did."

"What if I'm not ready?"

"I don't care," she said.

"Could I stay if I'm almost ready? If I was going to be ready soon?"

"No." My mother was emphatic. After she fell ill, she stopped saying that and talked about our staying together forever.

It's too soon, Mom, I thought as I watched her sleep. *I'm not ready yet.*

I went to school the next day, then played goalie in our after-school soccer match. The center forward for Redwood High was bearing down on me, racing toward the goal. We were behind, zero to five, in the second quarter, but then we were always behind when we played against Redwood. They had more players, more substitutes, more coaches. Worse—they were bigger, taller, and better than us.

I came out of the goal, determined to block her shot. People on the sidelines were cheering, but I could hear our coach shouting for me to stay back. The forward kicked, shooting the ball up and over to my right. I dove, reaching up and out. My fingers grasped the ball, pulled it into my stomach as I fell. I curled myself around it. The forward was on top of me.

"Drop it," she said. She glanced quickly over her shoulder and then kicked me in the head.

I got up, clutching the ball to my chest. "Foul!" I yelled as I blacked out.

I woke up on my back. I was lying on the examining table in the doctor's office.

"Slowly," the doctor said. "You have another concussion. Your coach brought you here." He closed the office door and leaned against it, arms crossed over his chest. He frowned.

"Okay, listen to me, Becky, this is your *third* concussion this season," he said. "I know what's going on. I know your mother is sick, and I think you're deliberately trying to hurt yourself by playing goalie. I will not keep patching you up, so I'm giving you a choice—you can quit playing goal and play fullback, it's less dangerous, or you can quit the team altogether—that's it, those are your choices."

I looked at my hands.

"If you won't talk to me, then I want you to go see this therapist," he said. He scribbled down a phone number and handed it to me. "Call her, you need to talk to someone."

"I need someplace to go," I mumbled.

"I can't hear you."

I raised my head up. "I said, *I need someplace to go.* My sister came yesterday, and she said I can't stay with my mom anymore, that it's not healthy for me. My mom's friends are going to take care of her now."

"I think that's better—why don't you see your guidance counselor? In the meantime, I think this therapist can help you."

The next day we performed our monologues for the last time before auditions. I went last. The rest of the students sat in folding chairs or on the floor, and Mr. Caldwell sat behind his desk up on the stage, taking notes. He announced me: "Rebecca Wilson, performing a contemporary monologue from *Mourning Pictures*, by Honor Moore. She plays the part of Margaret, the daughter."

I stepped forward and spoke words I'd cut from the monologue I performed in front of Mom.

"Ladies and gentlemen, my mother is dying," I recited. "I don't believe in miracles."

At the end of my performance, I stared at my classmates, a few of whom were sobbing. Others sat silently, tears wetly streaming down their faces. Others still couldn't look at me.

Mr. Caldwell cleared his throat. "Very powerful, Becky," he said. "Very raw—but I'm not sure how much of it is acting. Let's meet after class and talk."

I turned and ran out of the room.

It was too much for my friends, my mother dying. They were teenagers, but then it was too much for me, as well.

But one girl helped me. Rosa. She followed me out of class that day.

"Wait," Rosa called and caught up to me. She touched my arm.

"I need someplace to go," I said. "I can't stay with my mom anymore."

"Maybe you can come and stay with me and my mom."

"Really?" I said. "I can?"

"I think so, I have to ask—it's kind of strange, but my mom's a Buddhist priest. I know that sounds really weird, but she is, and she loves to adopt people."

"Really?"

"Yeah, I don't tell very many people," she said. "But hey, *your mom's* dying, which is even weirder." We smiled. "Let me call my mom. Maybe you can come tonight."

Rosa and her mother lived in a house near the Muir Woods National Park, just down the road from the Zen Center's Green Gulch Farm and Monastery. *Please like me*, I thought as I walked toward the house. *Please, please like me, please take me in.* A shaggy white and brown dog came up to me, wagging her tail. I stroked her muzzle, and she licked my hand. Through the glass doors of their house, I could see a woman with short hair, watching me. I knocked on the door. She gestured for me to come in. The dog followed me inside and sat down next to me.

"You must be Becky," the woman said. "I'm Jane, Rosa's mother."

"Hi," I said and tried not to stare at her black robes.

"That's Daisy." The woman nodded at the dog. "I think she likes you."

"Hi, Daisy," I said, looking down at the dog.

Jane watched me for a moment. "Well," she said. "You look like you could stand to be a kid for a while."

15 · SAY GOODBYE

J OYCE LOOKED UP from her knitting and smiled as I quietly opened the door.

"Your mom is resting," she said. "A lot of people have been calling, your brother's flying in from Hawaii." She stood up and kissed me on the cheek. "Your mom wants to see you. I'll be here if either of you needs me."

Mom was lying on her side, her breathing fast and shallow. She turned to me. The whites of her eyes were yellow.

"Hello, my Becky," she said. "I woke up just in time to see you. I heard you have a place to stay, that's good." She paused and panted a little. "I can't take care of you anymore. You understand, don't you?"

I nodded.

"Good girl." She closed her eyes again. "Open that," she said, gesturing toward her nightstand. I pulled the drawer open. Inside, there were stacks of one-hundred-dollar bills. "Take it," she said. "You'll need money."

I took a couple of stacks.

"Wait, there's something else." She opened her eyes wide and grabbed my arm. "Your brother owes me money, from when I sold our house. He's coming—you need to get that money from him, it's for you. Make him give it to you, do you hear me?"

"Yes," I said. "I hear you."

I packed four paper grocery bags of clothes, underpants, shoes, and socks and carried them out to my mother's Ford Falcon. Then I packed Mom's favorite things: an empty bamboo birdcage, a Balinese mural of Hindu gods, a green Javanese vase, a carved wooden Buddha, the sweater I'd crocheted for her when I was eight, home movies of Penny dancing, her unfinished master's thesis, her capes and dresses, her jewelry box, her "respectable mother-in-law wig" in its pink purse-shaped case, and the huge picture of my dad and Jack London.

From the bathroom shelf, I took her favorite piece of jewelry, a thick silver chain my father bought her in Mexico. On the chain hung an antique sterling silver Boy Scout badge, a bald eagle with its wings spread and a banner across its chest that read BE PREPARED. I put the necklace around my neck and headed to the car.

I crammed everything in and backed slowly out of the driveway, with the headlights off, so that the bright lights of the car wouldn't flash through the windows and burn my mother's eyes.

Friday they came for me, during Psychology class. Someone knocked. Mr. Downs rose, opened the door, and stuck his head out. He whispered to the person in the hallway. When he came back in, he looked at me.

"Becky, there are some people here to see you. I think you'd better come outside."

My sister stood in the hallway. Her friend Sally, who'd driven Amalia down, stood behind her. Amalia took a step toward me and stopped.

"It's time. Mom's dying, we need to go right now."

Facing each other across the hallway, we sobbed.

"Come on," Sally said gently. She stepped between us and put one arm around Amalia and the other around me and pulled us toward her. "C'mon, now, we can do this," she said, hugging and softly rocking us. "Let's go say goodbye."

In front of the high school was a green MG convertible parked in the fire lane.

Amalia and I climbed into the jump seat and sat up on the back of the car.

"Wait," Amalia said as we pulled into traffic in front of the high school. "We can't go like this—look at us—we look like shit. We need sunglasses."

"Of course," Sally said. "And flowers, lots and lots of flowers for Barbara."

Inside the five and dime in Mill Valley, Amalia put on a pair of pink heart-shaped sunglasses. I chose a pair of Elton John–style shades, square and studded with blue rhinestones.

"Our mother is dying," Amalia said to the clerk behind the counter. She took out a twenty-dollar bill and laid it on the counter. The price tag on her sunglasses bobbed as she talked. "We'll take the glasses. And lipstick, do you have any pink lipstick? Thank you. Here, Becky, you need a little color."

As we climbed back into the MG, Sally handed us two bouquets of pink and red roses, surrounded by white baby's breath and ferns. She sped out into the street. "Hold on," she shouted.

Amalia and I clutched the bouquets to our chests and held on to our sunglasses. A car honked at us. And then another.

"Wave," Sally said. "They want you to wave. They think you're the *homecoming queens, that this is the parade!*" She started honking back.

Tears streamed down Amalia's face. "Wave for Mom."

I waved slowly and then faster and faster.

"Mom," I yelled out. "Mom, wait! We're coming."

The house was crammed with old friends and neighbors from Bolinas. Lee's girlfriend, Jasmine, and their toddler were there, too. Lee stood in the living room, weeping and arguing with the doctor.

"Just give her an overdose of morphine," Lee said. "You're already giving it to her, just give her a big shot. I can't stand seeing her like this."

"No, your mother is not a dog to be put down," the doctor said. "I will not overdose her just because you can't handle the fact that she's dying. I know this is very painful for you, but it is her own death—you have to let her die her own way, in her own time. I will not let you take that away from her."

Annie appeared out of the crowd and took my arm. "Come, come see your mom," she said.

Annie, Amalia, and I walked toward my mother's bedroom. The room was crowded, dark, and hushed. The circle of people opened to let us through. In our sunglasses and lipstick, we moved toward my mother, the flowers still in our arms. Mother lay on a sheet, dressed in a white cotton tank top and green-flowered underpants. Her ribs moved quickly in and out, in and out, as she breathed.

Her eyes were shut. Behind her eyelids, her eyes rolled from side to side and up and down. She ground her jaw and grimaced, her body radiating heat, as if she were burning up from the inside out. Her breasts were hard and immobile under the thin cotton of the tank top, which was stained with a darkish fluid. The skin was taut over every bone. When she twitched, you could see the muscles flex in her arms and legs. The room was hot and smelled of sweat and the sweet stink of my mother's sickness. Stewart sat in a chair at the foot of the bed, lightly stroking her feet. Joyce sat by her head, a folded, damp washcloth in her hands. My mother frowned, shook her head. She appeared to be listening to someone only she could hear.

"No," she said, suddenly and clearly. "I'm not ready. Come back later."

Her eyes flew open, and she looked wildly around the room. Annie sat down beside my mother and gently stroked her hand.

"It's okay, Barbara. I'm here. We're all here," Annie said. My mother quieted.

We sat in the hot room, waiting, listening to her strained breathing. After a little while, she opened her eyes again. She frowned and clutched at the sheets.

"What are you all doing here?" she asked. "I'm not *dressed*. Does everyone have something to eat?"

Joyce wiped her forehead with the washcloth. "Yes, Barbara, we're all fine."

It was dark when she finally spoke again. "I'm ready, I'm ready to go now. Let me go—I want to go now. Please, let me go."

"Take your time," Annie said. "We have time."

I watched the rise and fall of her chest. Up, down. Up, down. Up, down. I couldn't breathe. There was not enough air in the room. *I'm too late*, I thought. *I shouldn't have left. She doesn't know me anymore.* I backed away from the bed. The circle of people closed around my mother, filling in the place where I had stood.

I SAT ALONE in Jane's house, waiting for the news that my mother had died. Two days before, Rosa and Jane had gone to New York for a three-day conference on American Buddhism.

"I hate leaving you here alone," Jane had said. "I can cancel—if you think your mother might die."

"No, she won't die," I said. "Yet."

"Do you want me to come and meet her before I go?" Jane had asked.

"No, thanks," I said. "Maybe when you get back we could go see her. I can take care of Daisy. I'll be fine."

"Are you sure?" she had frowned. "Do you have anyone to call? Just in case."

"My boyfriend, Bruce—well, he's sort of my boyfriend. His father is a priest, too, Episcopalian, I think—I'm sure I can call them. I'm going to church with him Sunday."

Sunday morning the phone rang.

"Becky? This is Annie. I'm calling to let you know that your mom died a little while ago. She died in my arms. She died very peacefully. The room was filled with light, it was very beautiful. Stewart and Joyce and I were all with her."

"Okay," I said. "Thank you for telling me. Thank you for staying." I choked. "I couldn't—"

"It's okay, Becky. It's really, really okay. Is someone there with you?"

"My boyfriend is coming."

"Good, you shouldn't be alone right now. I have to go—there's things we still need to do here, your brother's arranging for the cremation of your mother's body. I love you very much."

"Okay, goodbye." I carefully hung up the phone, walked across the room, and punched a hole in the wall.

WHEN BRUCE DROVE up, I got in the car and said, "My mom is dead."

He took my hand. "What do you want to do?"

"Go to church, like we planned."

When we got to his father's church in San Rafael, the service had just started. I slid into the pew next to him and stared at the huge crucifix hanging above the altar. White candles were burning, and the choir was singing. I did not know the words, but the sounds were familiar and holy.

My mother and I used to sing carols like this, I thought. Christmas was the one time she didn't mind God at all. My mother sang carols with passion, her strong voice rising and falling with the crescendos, her eyes bright and happy.

I stood and walked down the aisle. People were lined up in front of me, waiting their turn. Mimicking others, I knelt down in front of the altar and opened my mouth. I wept. Gently, Bruce's father, the priest, placed the thin wafer in my mouth. Then—as he passed again—I took the cup of wine from his hand, sipped it, and choked on the wafer. He laid his hand on my head and gently stroked my cheek. His white robe, the candles, and the music all swam together.

JANE SAID I could stay with her for a while longer. She arranged for my mother's memorial to be held inside the old barn the Zen Center had converted into a *zendo*, or meditation hall. Lee was bringing the ashes from the crematorium. Amalia and her family were on their way. Grandma and Grandpa, Kara and Ruby and their families, Annie, and all of my mother's friends were coming, too.

Lee arrived first. He reached into the car and lifted out a white urn. "Here's the ashes, I bought the most expensive urn," he said, trying to smile. "It's marble."

I stared at the heavy urn and then looked back at Lee. He was wearing an old-fashioned-looking dark gray suit, with narrow lapels and cuffed trousers, that was several sizes too big for him. He pulled at the lapels of his coat and looked away.

"That's Dad's," I said. "You're wearing Dad's suit. Where did you get that?"

"I've been saving it," Lee said, looking away from me. "I saved them all." He started crying. "I'm going to take a walk," he said. "I gotta pull myself together."

As he walked away, Amalia and her family pulled into the parking lot. She got out of the car and strode over to me. Her face was tight. "Lee's in trouble," she said. "He beat Jasmine last night, broke her nose and a couple of ribs.

She's at a battered women's shelter. The cops are looking for him."

"Oh, that's just fucking great," I said. "Let's hope they don't find him until after the memorial."

Annie met us in the hall, where people were already taking off their shoes in preparation for entering the *zendo*. She hugged us. "Boy, do I need a cigarette." She smiled. "Do you think any of these monks smoke?"

A monk in black robes came over carrying a long white cloth. He nodded at us. "Which one of you is going to carry the ashes?" he asked gently.

"I am," I said.

He laid the white cloth out on a small table and took the urn from me. He set the urn in the center of the cloth and tied the corners over it. He picked up the urn and put it back in my hands and tied the loose ends of the cloth around my neck, like a giant sling. I cupped my hands underneath. It was very heavy.

"Jane will be leading the ceremony," the monk said. "She will talk about your mother and her life first. Then there will be a place in the ceremony where people can stand up and speak. Is that okay?"

We nodded. Lee came in and stood behind Amalia.

"Are you ready?" the monk asked. From inside the *zendo*, we heard the light, high sound of chimes. The monk nodded. "Please, follow me."

I went carefully down the steps, breathing in the incense that burned on the altar. A raised dais ran along all four walls. Black-robed monks sat cross-legged on black *zafu* meditation cushions, hands folded in their laps. The monks' and nuns' heads were shaven. The altar stood at the center of the room. On it were flowers, candles, and a picture of our mother. I set the urn on the altar and followed Amalia and Annie to our seats. As we settled ourselves on the *zafu*s, a female monk handed us each a large laminated sheet with text printed on it.

"We'll begin with the 'Great Wisdom Beyond Wisdom Heart Sutra,'" she whispered.

We nodded and stared down at the sheets.

A large monk behind us chanted, "*Ommm*." We all jumped. "*Ommm*," he sang again. Another monk banged on a gong. The monks chanted to the rhythmic beat of the gong:

"*Oh, Shariputra, form does not differ from emptiness, emptiness does not differ from form . . .*"

Amalia snorted, then put her hand over her mouth. Beside me Annie had started to shake with laughter. I looked straight ahead and tried to concentrate on the words:

"*Therefore in emptiness: no form, no feelings, no perceptions . . . no eyes, no ears, no nose, no tongue . . .*"

A bubble of laughter rose up from my chest. I tried to swallow it.

"No color, no sound, no smell, no taste, no touch, no object of mind . . ."

We rocked and snorted, tears streaming down our faces, as the monks sang on.

"No suffering, no origination, no stopping, no path, no cognition . . ."

After the memorial, our grandfather stumbled out of the *zendo*. During the last year of her life, my mother had refused to let her parents visit, so they'd not seen her before she died. He stood there in his socks, looking at the rows and rows of shoes. He had a hole in one sock from which his big toe was peeking out. His plaid shirt was buttoned up all the way to the collar, his pants hitched up high and belted tightly above his waist. He spotted his shoes and bent to pick them up.

I walked over and said, "Hi, Grandpa, this must be a hard day for you. Why don't you come over here with me and sit on the bench? It'll be easier to put on your shoes."

He clutched his shoes to his chest.

"Who are you?" he asked, staring into my face. "Am I supposed to know you?"

16 · PEANUT BUTTER AND JELLY

MY MOTHER DIED in 1980, a week before my senior prom, and two weeks before my high school graduation. After the memorial, Lee disappeared; he was hiding from the cops, but after Jasmine fled home to Australia with their baby and the charges were dropped, he surfaced again.

Lee gave me a used green Datsun B-210, $200 to buy a prom dress, and a gram and a half of cocaine for my graduation.

"I want you to have fun," he said. "But try to be smart."

I bought a 1940s silver dress with pearl buttons and six-inch silver heels that I could barely walk in. The night of the prom, I put on the dress and stood in front of the mirror. "The 1940s were a horrible time for women," my mother once told me, "but they made clothes to fit real women's bodies, dresses were designed with *curves*."

In a photograph on my dresser, my mother was the same age as I was, seventeen, also dressed for a dance. Our seventeen-year-old bodies were exactly the same: shoulders that curved forward as if to hide our large breasts, each small-waisted, each with hips that flared. I didn't want to be reminded of how much I might be like her, so I put the picture away, hiding it from myself.

Bruce picked me up, and we drove to the Fairmont Hotel on Mason Street in San Francisco. We had a fight on the way. He hadn't wanted me to bring the cocaine with me, but now knew I had. The prom was in the Fairmont's Tonga Room. A fake rainstorm sounded as the band floated out on a barge in the pool in the center of the room. The band launched into "Lady Marmalade," and the room erupted, everyone dancing, whooping, singing along with the band, "*Voo-lay-voo-coo-shay-avec-moi, ce soire!*" I walked away from Bruce, leaned against the wall, and watched.

I had the cocaine and a hundred-dollar bill inside a silver mesh bag that had belonged to my great-grandmother. In a little satin pocket was a tiny beveled mirror for checking lipstick. I had never had my own coke before, wasn't sure how to cut it, or how much was safe to snort, so I'd asked Ricky Taylor, a big dealer at Tam High, to help me.

"Sure," Ricky said. "If you give me some."

Across the dance floor, I saw him heading for a side exit. He caught my eye and slipped through the door. I waited a few moments and then followed him into an elevator. We rode up to the roof garden and stepped out.

We were on the top of the hotel on Nob Hill, above Chinatown and North Beach, looking out over the night-bright city, all the way to the dark waters of the Bay.

"Do you have it?" Ricky said.

"Yeah," I said, pulling the envelope and the mirror out of my bag. "And I've got the hundred-dollar bill to snort it with."

Ricky unfolded the envelope, dipped his finger in the powder, and licked it. "This is good shit," he said.

"Well, well, well," somebody said. "What do we have here?"

We wheeled to face two security guards, a woman and a man, both in blue rent-a-cop uniforms decked out with walkie-talkies and nightsticks on their hips.

I thought to fling my great-grandmother's little silver bag at the cocaine to knock it off the balcony. The female hit my arm just as I let go and the bag flew in the wrong direction and skittered across the floor.

"Nice try," she said. "Raise your hands."

Ricky raised his hands, too, then he stepped back into the shadows and bolted around the corner.

"Let him go," the male cop said. "We've still got her."

"You got any ID?" he said.

I nodded toward my bag. "In there."

He retrieved it and pulled out my driver's license, took his walkie-talkie off his belt, and read into it, reporting my name and arrest for possession of cocaine. *Great*, I thought. *My mother's dead, and now I'm going to jail.*

The walkie-talkie squawked back incoherently, and the cop smiled at me and switched it off. He moved toward the bindle of coke.

"Of course, seeing how it's your prom, maybe we can let this whole thing slide," he said.

He picked up the mirror and tapped the coke back into the envelope and folded the edges closed. "You know, you really should be more careful." He smiled and tucked it into his shirt pocket and put my driver's license and silver bag where the coke had lain. *All they want is the coke!* I realized. *They're going to snort it themselves.* His female partner let go of my arm.

"You're very lucky we were the ones who caught you," she said. "Enjoy your prom."

I fled back down into the Tonga Room. Someone touched my arm.

"Hey, Becky, remember me? Pete, from soccer."

Pete who tried to grab my boob on the soccer field our freshman year and hadn't spoken to me since. He gripped my arm tighter.

"I got something I want to say to you," he said. "You remember when you knocked me flat on my ass on the soccer field? I always wanted to tell you, that was *really fucking cool*."

"Yeah, it was," I grinned back. "You *so deserved it.*"

"Yeah, I know," he said, and then his face fell. "Hey, sorry about your mom."

Later, Bruce and I made up, and I danced wildly and drank way too much.

A FEW DAYS later, I waited for my brother outside the Depot Café in Mill Valley. At my insistence, we were going to see an attorney about the money he owed to Mom's estate. Her will divided her estate into thirds, one third for each child, and Lee, surprisingly, generously, said he wanted to give me his third. But he wanted something in return, and we were to meet with my attorney to talk about terms.

Lee drove up in his silver Porsche. He got out and handed me a paper grocery bag. "Open it," he said.

The bag was filled with hundred-dollar bills.

"That's eight thousand. You hold on to that while we go talk to your attorney. You take care of me—I'll take care of you."

At the attorney's office, I held the bag on my lap while Lee and the attorney talked: He wanted to launder some other moneys through the estate by overstating the value of the estate. He would pay these moneys to me, and I would, in turn, give the moneys back to him.

"I think Becky and I need to discuss this in private," the attorney said. "Would you give us a moment?"

"Sure," Lee said. "No problem."

Lee stepped out of the room, and I took the money out of the bag and handed it to the attorney.

"He gave me this, and when I say I won't sign his papers, he'll take it away from me."

The attorney calmly took the cash and tucked it inside a drawer. "I think you might be right," he said.

"I know I'm right," I said.

When Lee came back in, he said, "Everything okay?"

The attorney cleared his throat. "Your sister says no. She thinks there might be papers somewhere in your mother's things that show the actual original amount of money loaned to you. Becky would rather wait to see if that's true before we agree to anything."

Lee blinked. "Why don't we just let it go for the moment?"

When we were outside, he said, "Get in the fucking car, and don't say a word."

I got in, holding the empty paper bag. He slammed the Porsche into gear and headed for the Golden Gate Bridge.

"I can't believe you embarrassed me in front of that guy," he said. "Who do you think you are?"

I covered my ears with my hands. We were speeding across the bridge; even with the wind and my hands over my ears, I could hear him ranting. We shot across the bridge and headed into the City. He swerved the Porsche into a parking place in the Marina. "Get out of my car," he said.

When I didn't move, he got out, ran around to the passenger side, and pulled the door open. "Give me the money."

I climbed out and faced him. "I don't have it," I said.

"What?" He grabbed the bag out of my hand and opened it. "Where is the money?"

A window opened in the apartment house behind my brother, and a man stuck his head out to peer down at us.

"I gave it to the attorney," I said.

My brother raised his fist.

I looked up at the man in the window. He had kind, watchful eyes.

I took a deep breath. "I knew you would try to take it back," I said. "But it's mine."

Lee was furious and made to hit me.

"Go ahead," I said. "Hit me, I don't care. Someone will call the cops, and I'll call the FBI."

"If you do that," Lee said, "I'll kill you. I can have you killed."

His words hung between us. Neither of us moved.

And then I laughed. "What would Dad say? What would he say if you killed me?"

Lee lowered his fist and turned away.

I started to laugh again as he walked away from me, then I couldn't stop laughing.

He did give me the money in the long run. For a while, he made monthly payments, then he'd stop, and we'd fight, but eventually he paid it all. It took ten years.

I WONDER SOMETIMES what my mother thought would happen after she died. I gather reasons why she did not have a plan for me. I try not to whine or glorify, try to be loving, but not pretend it was fine. I think they call this forgiveness.

I vacillate. Sometimes I love her as if she were my child, wide and forever. Sometimes I think if she were not dead, I'd kill her myself.

Mom did not love herself much. She was at her best, her most loving and courageous, as a friend, an ally. She came into her own in defiance, in defense of others. Perhaps she felt I did not need fighting for, that I was capable and strong. I am. But I'm also often secretly desperate. I am like her—anxious and self-doubting, wrapped in flash and bravado. I can't imagine why we thought I'd be anything else.

My mother raised me to be her friend, and in this, we were lost. I fantasize meeting my mother for tea. I get as far as sitting down at the table, and then I go blank. What would we talk about? Politics, literature, art, ideas. I would not say what I wanted to: *You had no plan for me. I was still a child. I hadn't yet grown up.*

Some days I find my mother in strange places. When I sing to my wolf-dogs, when I am kind to a child, and sometimes when I feel my own courage. On these days, my conversation with my mother is softer; I give us room.

I AWAKEN. It's late, and the room is dark. Jane and Rosa, my rescuers, are not home. I'm alone.

Earlier today, I'd tried to find my old horse, Shaheia, driving out to Point Reyes, looking for the rancher we sold her to, but I couldn't find him. I knocked on the doors of all the places nearby, but no one remembered my bay mare or the man who bought her.

The memory rises inside me, a bubble. I'm little again, and my mother and I are swimming in a pool. I cling to her shoulders, my hands placed exactly over the black straps of her one-piece bathing suit. The skin near her neck is hot, untouched by the water. I float behind her as she slowly breaststrokes from one side of the blue pool to the other. She hums softly and tows me along, and I am humming along with her, also counting the dark moles sprinkled across her back and shoulders. I draw invisible lines, connecting the dots with my fingers. When she turns at the end of the pool, she kicks hard once and we sink a little. I clutch at her.

"Don't hold on to me so tight," she says. "Let the water do it. The water itself will hold you."

Now, I feel I cannot breathe. In the dark room, my mother's spirit sits on my chest, crushing me. She's crying, "You don't love me, Becky. You don't love me anymore."

"I should have died with you," I say aloud to her. "I want to die."

I roll out of bed, pull on my clothes, and stumble out of the house. I skirt the Datsun B-210 and head for my mother's Falcon. Blind with tears, I fumble with the keys. *If I can just get to Annie*, I think, *I'll be okay. Her father died, too. She knows how I feel.*

I start the Ford, flick on the headlights, and head for Bolinas. The backseat of the car is still filled with my mother's things. Above Stinson Beach, I speed around a curve on the wrong side of the road and scrape the car against the metal guardrail, sparks flying off. A car comes at me around the corner, swerves, stalls, its horn blaring. I brake, jerk the steering wheel to the right, fly around the car. The birdcage falls over, and the pink wig box is tossed into the windshield and pops open, dropping the wig on the seat beside me.

"Annie, Annie, Annie," I chant. "Annie, Annie, Annie." My teeth are chattering.

In Bolinas, I speed across the Mesa and down the pot-holed dirt road to Annie's cabin. The house is dark, but the door's unlocked. *She must be at the bar*, I think. It's almost midnight—Smiley's closes at two. She'll come home then. I go inside, turning on the lights.

The large one-room cabin is a jumble of dirty clothes, manuscripts, old newspapers, dog-eared paperbacks, stacks of library books, a typewriter, and a sink full of unwashed dishes. I move some things off a chair, sit down. Then I stand up. I go to the fireplace and look at the photos on the mantelpiece.

Mixed in are old condolence cards from her father's death, less than a year ago, dried flowers, and little piles of beach agates. Also a clear glass urn of ashes. "Oh, no," I say, stepping backward.

I fumble through the stacks of paper on Annie's desk, looking for the phone. I punch "0" for the operator.

"C'mon, answer," I say. "Answer the phone."

"Operator, what city please?"

"I don't know. May I have the number for Suicide Prevention?"

"Hold on, honey, I'll put you through."

"Suicide Prevention, this is Beth. Hello? Who's there?"

I clear my throat. "Hi, um, I think—I'm afraid—I think I might kill myself."

"What's your name?"

"Becky."

"Hello, Becky, can you tell me why you want to kill yourself?"

"My mom just died," I say. "She had breast cancer."

"Becky, I'm so sorry—how awful for you. How old are you, Becky?"

"I'm seventeen."

"That's not very old. Where are you right now?"

"I'm waiting for my friend. I'm at her house. She'll come back soon—I just need to talk to someone till she gets here."

"We can talk as long as you need to. I have to ask you this—do you have any weapons? Have you taken anything at all? Any pills, or booze?

"No, nothing like that, I just want to die."

"Everything you're feeling is really normal when someone dies, especially when a parent dies. You're very young to have your mother die."

"I'm not that young. I took care of her myself, you know. Almost all the way. For a whole year," I say. "But I didn't do a good enough job because she died."

"Oh, I see—you feel like you should have saved her."

"Yes," I say. "I should have saved her."

The front door opens, and Annie walks in. Her eyes are bloodshot, her hair standing on end. She's smoking a cigarette. She sees me, exhales, smiles.

"Hi, Beck," she says.

"I have to go now," I say into the phone. "My friend's here now. Thank you."

"Who were you talking to?" Annie asks, stubbing out her cigarette in an empty cat food can.

"Oh, nobody. Just Suicide Prevention."

"Good girl," Annie says. "You hungry? Let's eat."

Annie opens the refrigerator and peers inside. "I only have peanut butter and jelly and some kind of weird, stale, organic-seeded bread from the Bolinas Co-op."

She pushes some dirty dishes aside, lays out the jars and the bread, and starts making sandwiches.

"Here, let's get in bed, where it's warmer, and eat."

She lays her sandwich on a pillow and pulls off her jeans. Her blue and pink flowered underpants have holes gaping at the waistband, where the elastic has pulled away from the fabric. I set my sandwich on the floor and pull off my shoes, then my pants, and I crawl into the rumpled bed beside her. We eat. We stare up at her father's ashes.

"That's my dad in there," Annie says, waving her sandwich. "I keep him here because I miss him. I talk to him all the time." She looks at me.

"It's the worst thing in the world to watch someone you love die. It's horrible and scary, especially when there's nothing you can do to help them. Pretty soon, they're so sick and in so much pain, they're not even the person you remember, the one you loved."

I say nothing. Annie goes on.

"It was awful, watching his mind fade away. He was so brilliant, and funny. I know he hears me when I talk to him. I drink too much and I smoke and cry."

I wipe my mouth on my sleeve and curl up beside her.

"It was easier for me being with your mom because she wasn't my mom. I'm not going to lie to you, Becky. You've lost *both* your father and mother, it's going to be really hard. You're going to be sad for a long, long time."

Then Annie sighs, slides down, and wraps her arms around me.

"Someday, I hope it'll get better," she whispers. "I think it will. But right now? I wouldn't count on it."

I close my eyes, leaning into her. Silently, we pull the covers up over our heads and listen as it starts to rain.

17 · LUCKY AND GOOD

Sometimes I imagine my first life; that is, the life I might have had if my father had not been murdered.

I'm grown up. My husband and I live in San Francisco in a brown shingled house where wisteria hangs over our front door—we are surrounded by books and classical music. I'm *successful*, a professor, or a political campaign manager. I wear expensive Italian pumps, my hair in a twist. We are in demand, so our phone rings all the time. My father likes my husband, who honors and respectfully defers to my father.

Or I'll imagine it another way: My mother leaves my father; there's a horrible divorce. My mother runs away with a teacher, or a gardener—some softer, less loud man, who takes up less space on his side of the bed. After Mom leaves, my father drinks too much and has a series of short-term affairs. My sister performs with the San Francisco Symphony in a beaded, low-backed gown. Amalia is regal, coveted. I am a jazz dancer. I have strong legs, a strong back, a long braid of hair.

In both versions my brother is an attorney, as our father wanted him to be. Lee's married, harried, and he works long hours, staying late at the office. He surfs on the weekends. He's a great dad, fixing his kids' bikes. He takes adult education classes in modern poetry. He writes poems on fresh yellow legal pads.

When my sister and brother were growing up in the nearly all-black neighborhood of the Fillmore District in San Francisco, Dad took Amalia into the alley to teach her how to box.

"Always stay on the high side of the street," he told her, "to keep the advantage." He showed her how to punch down—my sister hated that, but I'd have loved it.

Before leaving for school, Amalia rolled up the waist of her plaid school skirt to show off her legs. Every day, Dad rolled it back down. He would have rolled mine down, too.

I imagine myself as special, and that Dad and I would not have fought about the dishes or walking the dog or homework or the boys who aren't really good enough for me, or drugs or drinking or my staying out too late. I imagine arguing politics with him. I imagine that we're alike: dark-haired and blue-eyed, that we both pound the table with our fists, both of us heated and flushed with the joy of debate. I am a warrior, my father's girl.

In my favorite dream, it's early morning. Dad and I sit at the kitchen table together; we've made our separate breakfasts. We sit quietly. The sun pours in the window, I hear my father breathing; it's only an ordinary day.

But all this is the hunger of loss. I know who my father was: handsome, charming, charismatic, outrageous, brilliant, and at times, violent.

Sometimes I imagine my dad in heaven, sitting with Malcolm X, Martin Luther King, Jr., Che Guevara. They're drinking whiskey, playing cards, smoking fine Cuban cigars, and they're saving a seat for Fidel.

My fantasy for my mother is simple: that she'd get well, that I'd get to know her as I grew up, that she'd get to know me. After Dad is murdered, we stay in San Francisco instead of fleeing. Lee and Amalia and I grow up surrounded by people who knew him, so we can bask in the pride of being Dow Wilson's children. We three are close; we watch each other's backs. His murder does not destroy us.

In all these scenarios I am the same. I make mistakes, but I am confident. My father loves me, and I belong in the world. I am both lucky and good.

After high school, in real life, I knock around four colleges in San Francisco and then win a scholarship to transfer to Scripps College, a private women's college in Claremont, thirty-three miles east of Los Angeles. I take it and the hefty loan package that is part of the deal, and I set off south for

Claremont. When I'm unpacking in my dorm room, a girl who drives a red Mercedes asks me, "How much money does your daddy make?"

Stick to the high side of the street, I think, *and pick your ground.*

"I don't have a daddy," I say. "Do you want to fight?"

IT's HARD TO talk about murder. People react strangely: They're frightened and *very* curious. Mostly, they behave as if this kind of thing might be contagious, and they push us away. People can be *awful*. A meditation teacher who believed in past lives once said to me, "You must have done something really terrible in your last life to have had your father murdered in this life."

As siblings, Amalia, Lee, and I have struggled to find words, to find people who can listen. We can barely speak to each other about Dad's assassination. Mostly, we cannot help each other—the trauma ricochets among us; it's too much. Whatever peace we've each come to is separate, private.

In one of our rare conversations about Dad's death, Amalia once wished out loud that she and I could talk to the daughters of Malcolm X and Martin Luther King, Jr. We sat and wondered what their lives were like, what they did to survive. We wanted not to be alone with the sacrifice and brutality.

But I've found comfort in unexpected places. I taught a summer-long creative writing class for really poor kids at

Upward Bound, an educational equity program, at Oakland High. The city of Oakland has high poverty and murder rates, and my students were mostly African Americans, Latinos, Southeast Asian immigrants. My students called me "Miss Rebecca."

I instructed them, "Write about your first experience of love. Write about your first experience of death." When I said my father had been assassinated for political reasons, they surrounded me; they touched my hands, my face. They knew murder from their own experiences of the streets and through war in their homelands. With them, I was un-orphaned, no longer alone, and I cried.

I GOT MY wolves when I was thirty. Two wolf-dog pups— half-wolf, half-dog. Male and female. The male, Max, had a white face and golden eyes. He was black, silver, and tan. I named the bright-eyed female Chau, meaning "precious" in Vietnamese. Her coat was mostly black, with a patch of white on her chest and tan markings on her legs.

The pups were eight weeks old—they came home in a shoebox. At night, I put them in a carrier at the foot of the bed and slept with my feet at the head and my hand in the cage, touching them. When they were fully grown, Chau weighed eighty-six pounds, Max nearly a hundred. They felt like home, protective, warm, loving, safe.

I once took them to Muir Beach to visit my dad's ashes. The overlook was deserted, and we scrambled through the bushes, up to the rocks. I decided to sing for Dad, but my singing made Chau yip and howl, and I laughed instead.

My wolves loved the beach. We'd pile into the car with all their gear—water bottles, water dish, snacks, leashes, ratty dog towels I'd bought at yard sales—and drive Shoreline Highway along the coast to Muir Beach, or Stinson. Each trip began with a ritual: Once on the beach, I unleashed them, threw up my arms, and yelled, "Go play!" They raced into the water and then ran in ever-widening circles, Max loping and grinning, Chau, born with bad hips, a little slower, but determined to keep up.

Later, she dug little dens in the sand and dragged huge pieces of driftwood through the waves. Max sometimes trailed small canines that looked suspiciously like prey, freaking both the dogs and their owners out. I'd wave, smile cheerfully, and call him back to me.

If it was hot, I'd build a shelter of scratchy driftwood boards and an old sheet I'd packed, and when they were tired, we'd settle under the shelter and picnic. Raw turkey dogs for them, a sandwich for me, potato chips for all. On the ride home, they were wet, sandy, and content, and they slept as hard as children.

THE WOLVES WERE five and I was thirty-six when I met him. It was in a yoga class, and I was struggling into a pose when I felt someone looking at me, so I opened my eyes. An older man with glasses and a beard and mustache was smiling at me. I shut my eyes. When I opened them again, Malcolm was still there, and he was beaming.

It happened *every* time: I realized, *He likes me. He looks too nice*, I thought, peeking at him. *Old*, I thought, *but handsome.*

After yoga we hung out in the parking lot like teenagers, smoking American Spirit cigarettes. Gradually, we became friends. Malcolm was a therapist and an ex-Marine.

"Trying to get close to you is like circling a panther," he once told me.

One night, after a party at our yoga teacher's house, we sat on the porch under an arbor of roses and talked until late. Malcolm was very smart, funny, and unfailingly kind. I told him my story. Part of me wanted to scare him away, and the larger part wanted him to love me, but it was a shock that he actually did.

A few days later he told me, "I'm falling in love with you, Rebecca. If you don't want me to, I can stop, but I need to know soon."

"Can you wait just a little longer?" I asked.

"Okay," he said. "But hurry."

I called him later. "Here's the deal," I said, laying out the test. "If you want to keep on seeing me, you'll have to meet my wolves. If they like you, then we're on."

Chau was easy: She loved everyone, except loud, aggressive men and those who wore sunglasses and hats. But Max? Max was tough. He was aloof, picky.

The wolves and I were sharing a house near the Point Bonita Lighthouse, facing south, looking toward Lands End in San Francisco. I'd rented a room from a woman ranger who had three kids and a malamute—we were a rumpus of a household. In the winter, storms blowing in off the Pacific slammed our house, the waves hitting the cliff below us so hard, the house trembled. On these nights, the wolves and I huddled in bed together.

MALCOLM AND I agreed to meet across the estuary from Bolinas, on Stinson Beach.

The morning's clear and bright, the beach is empty. I'm jittery, but secretly hopeful. Behind Malcolm I can see the whole of Bolinas in the distance: the shore, the edge of town, and the Mesa above it, where I grew up. The swift channel between Bolinas and Stinson Beach glitters—the channel that I last swam across as a girl on horseback.

My wolves see him and lift their ears, as I hold my breath. Malcolm opens his arms, and suddenly, they are running toward him as if they *already know him!* They leap up and knock him over; his glasses fly; they all tumble into a heap, Malcolm at the bottom, laughing, Max and Chau on top, furiously barking, licking his face.

I watch them rolling in the sand and nod. *Okay*, I think, *this might actually work.*

When I approach my fortieth birthday, the fear begins. Dad died when he was forty. I suddenly get very anxious going to San Francisco, and this is a problem, because the consulting firm I'm working for is in the city and I'm commuting across the Bay by ferry from the Larkspur terminal, a mile west of San Quentin. Twice a day I travel between the two monumental markers of Dad's life, the Golden Gate Bridge and that prison. In San Francisco, whenever I'm close to South Van Ness Avenue, a frisson of fear splits my chest—I am just too close to the place he died.

For years Amalia and Lee have had trouble going to San Francisco, Amalia refusing to cross the bridge, Lee growing manic and crazy with grief whenever he's in the city. Now, it's happening to me.

Malcolm, the wolves, and I are living together. First, we lived in San Anselmo, in Malcolm's rented top-floor home in a funky, wooden house. Our kitchen consisted of a refrigerator, a sink, and a two-burner hot plate. The doctor who owned the house lived downstairs with her two children. The walls were so thin that Malcolm and I made love only when we knew no one else was home.

Malcolm is easy to live with. He's one of the happiest people I know. He celebrates me, and I find this wonderful, surprising.

Eventually we move in to a sunny cottage in Fairfax, tucked behind a large house, high above a creek. Our land-lord builds a ramp from the deck to the yard for Chau, so she can easily go up and down. Both across the street and down the hill are houses with huskies, and when the huskies howl, the wolves join in, filling the neighborhood with their voices.

MY GRIEF FOR my father comes late. It's wordless, feral. When it comes, I pull everything out of the closet, and I crawl inside. In that small darkness, I rock and pray, "Help me, help me," and "I'm okay, I'm okay." My wolf-dogs whine and scratch at the door. I stay there until it releases me, or Malcolm comes home and coaxes me out.

On impulse, I call San Quentin prison. I simply, suddenly *need* to know about Dad's murderers.

I dream of finding Rasnick: released from prison after serving only ten years, living in a suburban neighborhood, selling used cars, double-locking his door at night. As I arrive, his neighbors come out onto their porches to watch what will happen, not knowing they live next door to a murderer. I ring the doorbell. He answers, and as his wife hovers behind him, I ask: "Aren't you dead yet?"

A man answers the phone when I call the prison, "San Quentin prison." His voice is warm, efficient, and oddly welcoming.

"Can you help me? I'm trying to find out if the men who killed my father are still in prison, or if they're dead," I say.

"Hold on," he says. "I'm going connect you to someone in Victims' Rights—don't hang up."

The woman in Victims' Rights is also kind. She searches her database and finds that two are dead, and that the third disappeared after his release. From his date of birth, we figure he's probably dead as well. "I'm not supposed to do this," she says. "But let me give you their birth dates, in case you ever want to hire a private detective to confirm what I've told you."

I hang up, get up whooping, running from room to room, jumping on the bed, the couch, leaping onto the seats of chairs. Max and Chau chase me, barking and leaping.

When Malcolm comes in, carrying groceries, the wolves and I are still howling and jumping up and down on the couch.

"What the hell is going on?" he asks.

"They're dead!" I shout, waving my arms over my head. "They're *all dead! All* dead! They're *dead!* They're *dead!*"

BUT AS THE anniversary of Dad's death draws near, my grief grows. I will soon turn forty and will have outlived him. My father missed most of my life; we nearly missed one another completely. But every day, when I look in the mirror, I see him in my face. Myself: This is as close to him as I can get.

Then I hear there's a mural of my father in the old Labor Temple in San Francisco.

"Malcolm, I need to go see that mural," I say. "I want to go, but I just can't," I say.

He stands up from the table. "Let's go," he says.

"Right now?"

"Right now. I won't let anything happen to you."

I try to smile. "Okay," I say. "But I might throw up on you."

In the clippings about Dad, we find the addresses of the Labor Temple and the adjacent bar where my father had been the last night of his life, and we drive to the Mission District, to the cross-streets of Sixteenth and South Van Ness, a place my mother had never been able to take me. We park. We sit in the car, holding hands.

"Whenever you're ready," Malcolm says.

We sit quietly for a few more minutes.

"Okay," I finally say. "Let's do this."

Outside on Sixteenth Street, the crackheads twitch their way up and down the street, begging from passersby. Moving among them, we retrace my father's steps the night of his murder. First, we stand outside what had been the B&E Tavern on Sixteenth, where Dad had a drink with several of his men—the name is now changed, but it's still a bar.

"Do you want to go in?" Malcolm asks.

"Nah, it's just a bar." We then move slowly down the street, crack addicts giving us a wide berth. No one begs. "Why aren't they bugging us?" I ask.

Malcolm smiles. "Because they somehow *know*."

One man shivers and jerks toward me, catches my eye, nods, "How ya doing today?"

"Okay," I say. "I'm fine."

"You look good," he says.

The old Labor Temple building has become a theater, divided into small artists' studios. The mural of Dad is in the lobby. It covers the back wall from floor to ceiling.

He stands in an archway, dark-haired and bearded, dressed in his red sweater and jeans. He's wearing sandals. I know from Amalia this modern detail is wrong, that our father *always* wore black wing tip shoes to work.

His arm is raised, finger pointing as he banishes Rasnick. Four angry union men are in the street: one black, the others white. The black man also points at Rasnick, and Rasnick pulls at the man's sleeve. Reproductions of newspaper headlines and stories about the murder ring my father. The figure is big, his proportions heroic.

We consult our notes, trying to locate exactly where my father was killed. Malcolm talks to an older, more lucid-looking wino.

"Excuse me, sir, how long have you lived here? Do you remember anything about the murder of a labor leader that happened here, back in 1966?"

"No, man, sorry. I only got here in 1970 or so . . ."

We talk to a woman who runs the front desk of an auto repair shop on South Van Ness.

"I don't know," she says, "but my boss might. He owned this shop back then. He'll be here on Monday, if you'd like to come back."

I'm embarrassed. I pull on Malcolm's sleeve. "C'mon," I say. "Let's go."

On the street again, I hop from foot to foot. "This is not the right direction," I say. "It's on the other side, I can feel it." I point east, across the street. "That way."

We cross through the Sunday morning traffic. We're walking slowly, side by side, and reading off the numbers on the buildings, comparing them to the address I clutch in my hand, that of the barbershop that had its windows blown out by gunshots.

I stop in front of what is now a car dealership. "I think this is it. He was parked right here. He had his car keys in his hand."

I step into the street. Cars drive past me, around me. I turn, look east, up into the sky.

When I was a girl, I dreamed of my father flying up into the sky, very fast, disappearing as I tried to catch up.

Suddenly, I am not only calm, I am certain. I point to a patch of blue sky.

"Right there," I say. "He went out right there."

I look down for bloodstains. There is only oil and dirt. This was where my father left the world.

I feel my dad above me, around me. We pulse together and stand, joyous and steady, on that cracked and dirty pavement.

I smile. "Hello, Dad," I say.

"Are you all right?" Malcolm asks.

I look at him. For a moment he seems very far away, then I reach out and touch his arm.

"Yes," I tell him. "I'm okay."

I stand where my father died, and I do not break.

ACKNOWLEDGMENTS

THIS BOOK ENDURED innumerable stops and starts and took several forms before emerging. It would not exist without the help of many people who contributed to its completion.

Profound thanks to my terrific editor and publisher, legendary Jack Shoemaker, for embracing this story and me, and making it all so much fun.

Thanks to the great people at Counterpoint Press: Managing editor Laura Mazer for making it all happen; copyeditor Elizabeth Mathews for her fine eye and meticulous work; and designer Anna Bauer for the beautiful, perfect cover.

I am deeply grateful to my editors: Wise and patient Neshama Franklin read multiple drafts and asked me for a picture of my family; Jane Cavolina gave great structural direction and saved me from my own cleverness; friend Juris Jurjevics asked me the hardest questions with great love and found the beginning; and brilliant, funny Jane Vandenburgh taught me to listen and helped me bring it home.

Thanks to Don Deane, editor and publisher of the *Great Western Pacific Coastal Post Newspaper*, where the idea began; the members of the Berkeley Tuesday Night Writers Group for prodding, Sanford Dorbin, Daniel Marlin, Christopher Miles, and Janell Moon; and my readers over the years, Annie Beradini, Ianthe Brautigan, Mary Bell, and Rosa "Little Fish" Jurjevics, and Janine Reid.

Gratitude to Betty Andrews, Nancy Bellen, Consuella Brown, Rob Hayden, Katherine Randolph, Lucinda Toy, and Ruth Williams, for insight and support while completing this manuscript.